I LOVE TO PREACH THE STORY:
FINDING OUR ROOTS IN GENESIS & EXODUS

*(SERMON SERIES BASED ON
OLD TESTAMENT READINGS IN CYCLE A)*

Rolf Svanoe

CSS Publishing Company, Inc.
Lima, Ohio

I LOVE TO PREACH THE STORY

FIRST EDITION
Copyright © 2023
by CSS Publishing Co., Inc.

Library of Congress Cataloging-in-Publication Data
Names: Svanoe, Rolf, author.
Title: I love to preach the story / Rolf Svanoe.
Description: FIRST EDITION. | Lima, Ohio : CSS Publishing Company, Inc.,
    2022- | Contents: Year A. Finding our roots : summer series preaching
    from the RCL Year A, a semi-continuous alternative Old Testament reading
Identifiers: LCCN 2022001112 (print) | LCCN 2022001113 (ebook) | ISBN
    9780788030468 (paperback) | ISBN 9780788030475 (adobe pdf)
Subjects: LCSH: Bible. Old Testament--Sermons. | Common lectionary (1992) |
    Worship programs. | Lectionary preaching.
Classification: LCC BS1151.55 .S93 2022 (print) | LCC BS1151.55 (ebook) |
    DDC 221.071--dc23/eng/20220511
LC record available at https://lccn.loc.gov/2022001112
LC ebook record available at https://lccn.loc.gov/2022001113

For more information about CSS Publishing Company resources, visit our website at www.csspub.com, email us at csr@csspub.com, or call (800) 241-4056.

e-book:
ISBN-13: 978-0-7880-3047-5
ISBN-10: 0-7880-3047-7

ISBN-13: 978-0-7880-3046-8
ISBN-10: 0-7880-3046-9

Printed in U.S.A.

CONTENTS

Preface 5

Chapter 1 – Why Tell Stories? 7

Chapter 2 – The Revised Common Lectionary And
The Old Testament 10

Chapter 3 – Preaching Stories Of Origin 13

Chapter 4 – The Story, The Sermon And The Song 16

Trinity Sunday – Genesis 1:1-2:4a
"In The Beginning" 16

Proper 4 / Ordinary Time 9 – Genesis 6:9-22; 7:24; 8:14-19
"A Rainbow And A Promise" 23

Proper 5 / Ordinary Time 10 – Genesis 12:1-9
"When God Calls" 29

Proper 6 / Ordinary Time 11 – Genesis 18:1-15
"Is Anything Too Wonderful For The Lord?" 33

Proper 7 / Ordinary Time 12 – Genesis 21:8-21
"God Hears Our Cries" 38

Proper 8 / Ordinary Time 13 – Genesis 22:1-14
"Making Deals with God" 43

Proper 9 / Ordinary Time 14 – Genesis 24:34-38, 42-49, 58-67
"Matchmaker, Matchmaker" 47

Proper 10 / Ordinary Time 15 – Genesis 25:19-34
"The Trouble With Twins" 53

Proper 11 / Ordinary Time 16 – Genesis 28:10-19a
"God Is Climbing Jacob's Ladder" 58

Proper 12 / Ordinary Time 17 – Genesis 29:15-28
"When The Trickster Got Tricked" 63

Proper 13 / Ordinary Time 18 – Genesis 32:22-31
"What's In A Name?" 68

Proper 14 / Ordinary Time 19 – Genesis 37:1-4, 12-28
"When Bad Things Happen"   **74**

Proper 15 / Ordinary Time 20 – Genesis 45:1-15
"The Power Of Forgiveness"   **82**

Proper 16 / Ordinary Time 21 – Exodus 1:8-2:10
"Disobeying Pharaoh's Command"   **88**

Proper 17 / Ordinary Time 22 – Exodus 3:1-15
"When God Hears Our Cries"   **94**

What Next?   **99**

Preface

The idea for this preaching series (and ultimately for this book) came from colleagues and staff at the church I was serving, Peace Lutheran in Sioux Falls, South Dakota. This was a large church with four pastors where I preached every third week. I enjoyed immensely preaching through these Old Testament stories and trying to make them come alive for the congregation. When I moved to a smaller church, I was faced with the challenge of preaching every week. I found that these stories continued to hold my interest and the interest of the congregation.

The sermons in this book are all mine, and I take credit and blame for them. I don't include them as examples of "good" sermons, but simply as showing possibilities for busy pastors struggling to preach the word week after week. Though I try to be faithful to that word, I realize that these sermons also grow out my background and worldview: white, middle class, male, Lutheran, liberal, and someone who finds great enjoyment in his Norwegian heritage. These sermons are personal and the stories in them are often personal, attempting to connect God's word to current events in our society in ways that can help make that word come alive today. I hope these stories will "prime the pump" and help the reader connect to her/his own stories and current events.

Thank you to the good people at Greenfield Lutheran Church in Harmony, Minnesota, who endured these sermons during the summer of 2017. That church was established in 1856 by Norwegian pioneers, a legacy still preserved by the church's biennial lutefisk supper. Somehow, they found the grace to put up with a pastor who was a Green Bay Packer cheesehead living among Minnesota Vikings fans. It was testimony to the power of the gospel that helped us to live with each other "in harmony."

Chapter 1

Why Tell Stories?

When summer approaches, one of the more mundane things preachers worry about is the slump in attendance and giving. For many churches, Sunday school is not in session. Weekend activities compete for family time. What can the church do to make summer worship more interesting?

Many pastors who are committed to the Revised Common Lectionary often preach on the gospel lesson. But pastors who have preached the three-year lectionary a few times around may be looking for other preaching material to peak their interest. That is when a closer look at the lectionary may suggest another option in the alternative semi-continuous first reading. During the time after Pentecost, the Revised Common Lectionary provides an alternative semi-continuous Old Testament reading each year. These are wonderful stories that aren't often preached on. Many of these stories are favorites for our people. They are the reason we sing the great hymn of faith, "I Love To Tell The Story."

People love to tell and hear stories. We are *homo narrans*, a story-telling people. Our world is shaped by the stories we tell, stories that help us make sense of our daily lives by giving us a larger metanarrative within which we can locate ourselves. Storytelling is one of the ways we bear the image of God. There is a wonderful quote by Elie Wiesel in the preface to his novel, *The Gates of the Forest*, where he said that "God made man because he loves stories." (Wiesel 1966). Our love for stories comes from God. And as the hymn says so well, God's story "satisfies my longings as nothing else would do."

There is something powerful about a story. A good story will draw us into its world and help us to identify with its characters. We begin to see ourselves in the story so that the story speaks to us and changes us. The worst thing a preacher can do is to distill the main point of the story and preach about a principle from an ancient past. Elizabeth Achtemeier warned us about this in her book, *Preaching From The Old Testament*.

Stories have the character of allowing us to enter into them. We identify with the figures in them and find them telling the story of our lives. And this is one of the functions of the stories in the Bible — they let us enter into their events, to experience and feel what has happened, so that the story becomes our story and the happening an event in our situation. What a difference it can make really to preach the stories, rather than distilling out of them eternal truths and principles![1]

Preach the story! Tell the story in such a way that the congregation sees itself in it.

As you prepare for your summer series, my suggestion is that you set aside a few hours and read through this whole book to get an overarching view of the series and its narrative flow. Let it inspire you to build on the series with your own ideas and creativity. Adapt it to your own context and current events. Tell your own stories. My stories will simply help you to connect to your own experiences. You will make this series even better. And when you go on vacation and a supply pastor comes in, share this book so they know how to fit into the summer series.

Pastors will want to give some thought how to tell each story. Because of the length of some of the stories, it can be valuable to present it as "Reader's Theater." Print the reading in the bulletin (or project it on a screen), and designate parts for the congregation to read. Assign the congregation a certain voice from the narrative. Include one or more other readers, depending on the demands of the story. This keeps the congregation involved and participating in some of the longer narratives.

Pastors may also want to consider the use of actors or props in telling the story. For instance, in the Year A Genesis 1 creation story, I had God dressed as a clown who used pictures and plants and stuffed animals to represent each stage of creation. Check out the video on my YouTube channel here: https://youtu.be/MLUDIZ_D7iI. You may want to consider putting together your

1 Elizabeth Achtemeier, *Preaching from the Old Testament*. (Louisville, Westminster/John Knox Press, 1989) p. 15.

own children's bulletin with questions to help families engage the story even further.

Along with the reading, I have also included hymn/song suggestions. Finding the right hymn or song to go with a text can take some time. Sometimes there are no obvious choices to complement a story. Hopefully these suggestions will save some time for busy pastors.

Each week will follow this pattern:
- The Story
- The Sermon
- The Song

My prayer is that this book will be the starting point for congregations to encounter these stories from the Bible. Use your own creativity and imagination to make these stories come alive for your congregation today. I hope at the end of the summer you will join me in saying, "I love to preach the story!"

Chapter 2

The Revised Common Lectionary

And The Old Testament

In assigning the Old Testament reading, the authors of the Revised Common Lectionary generally followed a principle called complementarity, meaning that the Old Testament reading is chosen to be a complement to the gospel reading. This is always the case during the festival half of the church year (Advent to the Day of Pentecost). However, during the non-festival half of the church year, the lectionary gives us two options for the first reading. One is to follow the same principle of complementarity as the first half of the church year. The gospel reading is the primary reading of the day, and the Old Testament reading is chosen to complement it.

Complementing happens in three ways. First, an Old Testament reading may be chosen because the gospel reading cites a passage from the Old Testament. For example, on the Second Sunday of Advent, the gospel reading has John the Baptist quoting from the prophet Isaiah chapter 40. Following this principle of complementing, the first reading then is Isaiah 40. The lectionary authors want us to know that without understanding the Old Testament context, we have a harder time understanding the New Testament.

A second way complementing happens is the Old Testament selection helps us to deepen our understanding of the gospel reading. So, for example, when Jesus talks about forgiveness in Matthew 18, the Old Testament reading chosen is from Genesis 50 where Joseph forgives his brothers. Another example is when Jesus teaches his disciples to be persistent in their prayers, the complementing Old Testament passage is the story of Abraham bargaining with God to save the people of Sodom and Gomorrah.

There is a third way complementing happens when the Old Testament reading contrasts with the gospel reading. The contrast helps us to understand more fully the gospel message.

10

One example of this is on the First Sunday in Lent when Jesus successfully endures temptation, we hear the Genesis story of Adam and Eve giving in to temptation. Contrast can often be an important way of understanding a New Testament text.

But during the non-festival half of the year, the lectionary authors see another way to complement the gospel.

> "Here, during Year A, semi-continuous selections from especially Genesis and Exodus are read. The idea is that, since Matthew relies so consistently on the tradition of Moses, during the year of Matthew these books are proclaimed. Similarly, since Mark describes Christ as the hidden Messiah (that is, the anointed one), the court histories that tell of the anointed kings of Israel are heard in year B. Since Luke's gospel shows such concern for justice to the poor, writings from the prophets are proclaimed during year C. The complementarity goes not Sunday by Sunday, but through the half-year.[2]

This alternative way of complementing the gospel takes a broader view of seasonal themes and theology, as opposed to a Sunday-by-Sunday correspondence. The advantage here is that by preaching on a semi-continuous series of texts, the preacher can develop an overall theme for the series and establish a direction and momentum throughout the summer.

There is another artificial way of viewing these three summers' series of texts. Year A focuses on stories of origin. We learn from the *past* who we are and where we come from. Year B focuses us on the lives of the rulers of Israel and the decisions they make in their daily lives. We learn from them how to live our lives in the *present*. Year C focuses us on the *future* consequences of our present actions. The prophets warn us to avoid disaster, or they give voice to our hopes and dreams for a better future. Past, present, and future find place in these three summers of series.

Most recently (2018), I have preached through the Year B stories of the kings of Israel. This has occurred at the same time as

2 Gail Ramshaw, *A Three-Year Banquet: The Lectionary for the Assembly.* (Minneapolis: Augsburg Fortress) p. 54-55.

a debate in the United States over the limits of presidential power and defining the abuse of that power. It was very noticeable how week after week these stories spoke in surprisingly relevant ways.

> The idea is that, granting Mark's emphasis on the surprising nature of Christ's kingdom, the lectionary in Year B should review the stories of the ancient kingdom of Israel. Thus the first readings for June through August in year B are the following narratives: the call of Samuel; Israel's desire for a king; the anointing of David; either the battle between David and Goliath or the friendship of David and Jonathan; David's lament at the death of Saul; David's consolidation of Israel and Judah; his dancing before the ark; God's rejection of David's hope to build the temple; David's sexual intercourse with Bathsheba; Nathan's confrontation with David; Absalom's rebellion; Solomon's prayer for wisdom; and Solomon's dedication of the temple. The advantage to this pattern is that if people attend church regularly, they will learn the legends of the Davidic monarchy.... The challenge is to maintain the focus on each Sunday as the celebration of Christ's resurrection.[3]

When preachers choose to work through the stories of Kings Saul, David, and Solomon, it can be especially insightful to draw a *contrast* between the behavior of these ancient kings and the nature of Jesus' kingship. Jesus did not come to be served, but to serve. "You know that the rulers of the Gentiles lord it over them, and their great ones are tyrants over them. It will not be so among you; but whoever wishes to be great among you must be your servant, and whoever wishes to be first among you must be your slave; just as the Son of Man came not to be served but to serve, and to give his life a ransom for many" Matthew 20:25-28. Not only can we draw contrasts between Jesus and David, but also between Jesus and current world leaders who abuse their power to serve themselves instead of their people.

3 Ibid.

Chapter 3

Preaching The Stories Of Origin

Have you seen the television commercials advertising DNA testing and learning your family history? They seem to be ubiquitous in the media and internet. There is a growing fascination with learning the story that our DNA can reveal about who we are and where we come from. Somehow, knowing that history helps to define us and give some focus to our lives.

The book of Genesis presents us with family stories of origin that reveal our spiritual DNA and help to shape our lives as people of faith. These stories tell us who we are and whose we are. Not only do they reveal something about us, but more importantly they reveal something about God and who God is. These stories define us and give direction to our faith and how to live our daily lives as people of God.

The stories presented to us in the lectionary's alternative semi-continuous first reading are some of the most beloved from our family history storybook. Creation, Adam and Eve, Noah, Abraham and Sarah, Hagar and Ishmael, Isaac and Rebekah, Jacob and Esau, Joseph, and Moses — these are the superstars in our summer blockbuster series. Fortunately for preachers, there is no dearth of commentary on these texts to help us interpret them for our congregations. These stories give rich fodder for exploring common family dynamics: discerning God's will in an uncertain future, finding an appropriate spouse, issues of infertility and pregnancy, raising children, and dealing with sibling rivalry. Amid all the family dysfunction, God's faithfulness is revealed. The message of these stories is clear: God is a promise maker and promise keeper.

How are we to preach these Old Testament stories? In his book, *Preaching from the Old Testament*, Old Testament scholar, Walter Brueggemann, encourages preachers to keep the historical context in mind in which the Pentateuch was written and edited. How did the narrative function in that context? Our contemporary Christian proclamation should function in much the same way.

Thus I suggest, for our thinking about Christian preaching, that just as the Torah, in its completed form in the Persian period, provided Jews with a distinct narrative identity in the face of Persian domination, so the preaching task from Genesis is the maintenance of baptismal identity in the face of the life authorized and limited by market ideology. The Torah that centers on the awesome power and the abiding fidelity of God provides standing ground outside the massive claims of empire. The Torah is a testimony to life outside the dominant hegemony of empire, and a tool for articulating and maintaining that "life outside."[4]

The stories of origin in the Pentateuch provide a master narrative to ground our identity and challenge any ultimate claims by market ideology or empire.

Elizabeth Achtemeier, in her book, *Preaching from the Old Testament*, encourages preachers to ask two questions: what is happening and what is the outcome?

By clinging to the narrative of the biblical history, by asking what is happening in it, and by inquiring what its outcome was in the total canonical context, we avoid turning the story into a timeless truth. We prevent the text from being moralistically applied to our lives, as some eternal principle. And we anchor the whole in the history which God in fact has brought about and in which we in fact now stand, as his new covenant people. We set our people in that real story, that great cosmic drama, that God is working out. Those are the questions to ask of every narrative in the Old Testament: What is going on in it and what was its outcome?[5]

4 Walter Brueggemann, *Preaching from the Old Testament*. (Minneapolis: Fortress Press, 2019), p. 8.
5 Elizabeth Achtemeier, *Preaching from the Old Testament*. (Louisville: Westminster/John Knox Press, 1989), p. 63.

Achtemeier gives several examples to show that the outcome will often find its greatest resolution in the story of Jesus.

Preaching these stories of origin can be very satisfying for both preacher and congregation. This series also is an excellent opportunity to address some of the larger issues facing our world today. What insight does the story of Noah bring to concerns of global climate change? Abraham is a common ancestor to three major world religions. Bruce Feiler has written sensitively about the way in which Jews, Christians, and Muslims have viewed these stories. His book, *Abraham: A Journey to the Heart of Three Faiths* (2005) could make for a wonderful book discussion. Another book, *The Faith Club: A Muslim, A Christian, A Jew — Three Women Search for Understanding* (2007) could also create helpful interaction. Lutheran Social Services of Minnesota has produced a helpful curriculum called, My Neighbor is Muslim: A Small Group Study Exploring the Muslim Faith. Including some of the insights from other faith traditions enriches our understanding of these texts and gives a timely reminder of the ways they bring us together. Explore the resources in your own community. Are there local persons who can speak to an adult forum about these other faith traditions? Another option is to view the video series on Genesis hosted by Bill Moyers for PBS that included Christians, Jews, and Muslims all interacting with the same story. With accompanying book/study guide this resource could be a helpful tool for hearing the stories of Genesis in new ways that require minimal preparation.

Congregations may want to offer a creative retelling of the story to the children each week in the children's message. One week the children could gather around a rocking chair and read the story from a Children's Bible storybook. Another week there could be a puppet show, a reader's theater, or a skit. Investing time in preparing a creative children's message will be time well-spent. Consider producing something families can take home with a few questions as conversation starters to dig deeper into the stories.

What makes this summer different from all other summers? These stories from Genesis can bring a renewed energy "to tell the old, old story of Jesus and his love."

15

Chapter 4

The Story, The Sermon And The Song

Trinity Sunday — Genesis 1:1-2:4a
"In The Beginning"

1. The Story. (The voice of God below is assigned to the congregation. However, if you are acting out the part of God with visuals, assign the voice of God to an unseen voice so that the congregation can observe the action.)

Reader: "In the beginning when God created the heavens and the earth, the earth was a formless void and darkness covered the face of the deep, while a wind from God swept over the face of the waters. Then God said,

All: 'Let there be light';

Reader: and there was light. And God saw that the light was good; and God separated the light from the darkness. God called the light Day, and the darkness he called Night. And there was evening and there was morning, the first day. And God said,

All: 'Let there be a dome in the midst of the waters, and let it separate the waters from the waters.'

Reader: So God made the dome and separated the waters that were under the dome from the waters that were above the dome. And it was so. God called the dome Sky. And there was evening and there was morning, the second day. And God said,

All: 'Let the waters under the sky be gathered together into one place, and let the dry land appear.'

Reader: And it was so. God called the dry land Earth, and the waters that were gathered together he called Seas. And God saw that it was good. Then God said,

All: 'Let the earth put forth vegetation: plants yielding seed, and fruit trees of every kind on earth that bear fruit with the seed in it.'

Reader: And it was so. The earth brought forth vegetation: plants yielding seed of every kind, and trees of every kind bearing fruit with the seed in it. And God saw that it was good. And there was evening and there was morning, the third day. And God said,

All: 'Let there be lights in the dome of the sky to separate the day from the night; and let them be for signs and for seasons and for days and years and let them be lights in the dome of the sky to give light upon the earth.'

Reader: And it was so. God made the two great lights — the greater light to rule the day and the lesser light to rule the night — and the stars. God set them in the dome of the sky to give light upon the earth to rule over the day and over the night, and to separate the light from the darkness. And God saw that it was good. And there was evening and there was morning, the fourth day. And God said,

All: 'Let the waters bring forth swarms of living creatures, and let birds fly above the earth across the dome of the sky.'

Reader: So God created the great sea monsters and every living creature that moves, of every kind, with which the waters swarm, and every winged bird of every kind. And God saw that it was good. God blessed them, saying,

All: 'Be fruitful and multiply and fill the waters in the seas, and let birds multiply on the earth.'

Reader: And there was evening and there was morning, the fifth day. And God said,

All: 'Let the earth bring forth living creatures of every kind: cattle and creeping things and wild animals of the earth of every kind.'

Reader: And it was so. God made the wild animals of the earth of every kind, and the cattle of every kind, and everything that creeps upon the ground of every kind. And God saw that it was good. Then God said,

All: 'Let us make humankind in our image, according to our likeness; and let them have dominion over the fish of the sea, and over the birds of the air, and over the cattle, and over all the wild animals of the earth, and over every creeping thing that creeps upon the earth.'

Reader: So God created humankind in his image, in the image of God he created them; male and female he created them. God blessed them, and God said to them,

All: 'Be fruitful and multiply, and fill the earth and subdue it; and have dominion over the fish of the sea and over the birds of the air and over every living thing that moves upon the earth.... See, I have given you every plant yielding seed that is upon the face of all the earth, and every tree with seed in its fruit; you shall have them for food. And to every beast of the earth, and to every bird of the air, and to everything that creeps on the earth, everything that has the breath of life, I have given every green plant for food.'

Reader: And it was so. God saw everything that he had made, and indeed, it was very good. And there was evening and there was morning, the sixth day. Thus, the heavens and the earth were finished, and all their multitude. And on the seventh day God finished the work that he had done, and he rested on the seventh day from all the work that he had done. So God blessed the seventh day and hallowed it, because on it God rested from all the work that he had done in creation. These are the generations of the heavens and the earth when they were created." Word of God, word of Life.

All: Thanks be to God.

2. The Sermon

When modern people hear the creation story they often ask questions like: Did God really create the world in six days? How does this story fit with modern science and the theory of evolution? We are often forcing the Creation story to answer questions it was never meant to answer. We want to know things like how God created the world and when? But the author wasn't interested in answering those questions. Instead, he wanted us to know *who* created the world and *why*? If we insist on reading this story literally, we read it in a way the author never intended. Did God really create everything in six days? It doesn't matter. What does matter is that we know that God created the world, and that God created it with design and purpose. And God finds joy and delight in the creation. We should, too!

Most scholars feel that this Genesis creation story was written during the Babylonian exile. God's people had been conquered. They watched as their homeland was destroyed and then were forced to march to Babylon and live as servants. It was a crisis of

19

faith for them. Where was God? Why did God let this happen? Did God care about them anymore? Maybe the Babylonian gods were more powerful? It was tempting to give up their faith in the God of their ancestors. The Babylonians had a creation story. They believed that the world came about through a war, one god slaying another and spreading the remains of the dead god's body across the universe to make the stars. In contrast, the author of Genesis 1 wanted to say that instead of an act of war and violence between many gods, there is one God who created the world out of love. Instead of a random scattering across the heavens, God created with purpose and design. These are two very different creation stories. Which story do you want to believe?

We have the same today. Some scientists want to tell us that the universe and the world we live in is the product of random chance. I don't know about you, but I think it takes more faith to believe that this is all the result of chance, than to believe that everything is the result of God's design. God may have used a process like evolution over billions of years, but still there is God's guiding hand in the process.

There are so many things we could talk about in this story. I think one of the significant things for us today is that we human beings are made in God's image. Both male and female bear God's image. God has both male and female characteristics, and so we shouldn't be surprised when sometimes we hear God referred to as she, or as our mother. So when you get up in the morning and stare at your face in the mirror, do you say, "Good morning, God!" or do you say, "Good God, it's morning!" You bear the image of God. Some of you might bear it a little better than others, but you all bear it. Remember that the next time you meet your neighbor you have a hard time getting along with. Remember that the next time you hear people calling for the destruction of our enemies. They too, bear the image of God.

A little girl was sitting on her Grandpa's lap. She held his hand and studied the deep wrinkles in his skin, tracing them with her finger. She looked up at him and said, "Grandpa, did God make you?" "Why yes, honey, God most certainly did make me a long time ago." The little girl thought about that for a while, and then asked her grandpa another question. "Grandpa, did God make me?" "Oh yes, dear, God made you a very beautiful little girl." The little girl thought about that some more, and then said to her Grandpa, "Grandpa, I think God is doing a much better job today."[6]

What does it mean that human beings are made in God's image? People have debated that over the years. Is it our ability to reason or our ability to think abstractly? Maybe to bear God's image is our ability to communicate? Could God's image be our capacity to love? What the author goes on to say is that to be made in the image of God is to have dominion over the creation. God brings order out of the chaos and invites us to share in that work of dominion.

But what does that mean, to have dominion? Several years ago, an environmentalist named Rachel Carson wrote an article called Silent Spring in which she blamed this creation story for much of the despoiling of our world and the pollution of the planet. Apparently, some interpret the charge to have dominion over the world as having the right to use and abuse the planet any way we want. But is that really what this means?

In the creation story, God brings order out of chaos, and gives human beings the same role to bring order out of chaos for the good of all. The word dominion is used to describe the role of the king in caring for his kingdom. The king is to overcome the chaos by bringing order and peace. Having dominion does not give the king permission to use and abuse his subjects any way he wants to gratify his own desires. That's exactly what King Solomon did and it destroyed the country. Listen however, to what the psalmist says in Psalm 72 about how the king should exercise dominion.

"Give the king your justice, O God, and your righteousness to a king's son. May he judge your people with righteousness, and your poor with justice. May he defend the cause of the poor of the people, give deliverance to the needy, and crush the oppressor. May he have dominion from sea to

6 Author unknown.

sea...For he delivers the needy when they call, the poor and those who have no helper. He has pity on the weak and the needy, and saves the lives of the needy. From oppression and violence, he redeems their life; and precious is their blood in his sight."

This is what it means to have dominion — to overcome the chaos of our selfish natures with justice and peace. God did this in the Old Testament by giving the Law. God does this in the New Testament by giving us his Son, Jesus Christ. God has dominion over us through love and forgiveness, through the death and resurrection of Jesus, God's Son.

In our baptism, we make promises on behalf of our children. Listen again to these words. "As you bring your children to receive the gift of baptism, you are entrusted with responsibilities: to... nurture them in faith and prayer, so that your children may learn to trust God, proclaim Christ through word and deed, care for others and the world God made, and work for justice and peace."[7] That sounds an awful lot like dominion language to me — to care for others and the world God made, and work for justice and peace. When you work to make the world a better place, you exercise dominion and live out your baptism. That happens when you work to overcome injustice and resolve conflict, when you care for the environment, when farmers care for their land and seek to improve it for future generations, when we reduce our carbon footprint to fight climate change, when we do these things we exercise dominion and live out our baptism.

The stories of Genesis aren't just ancient myths. They are God's word to us today, calling us to love and care for God's creation and to participate in God's work of justice.

3. The Song — "God Who Stretched The Spangled Heavens"

---

7 *Evangelical Lutheran Worship* (Minneapolis: Augsburg Fortress, 2006), p. 228.

Proper 4 / Ordinary Time 9 — Genesis 6:9-22; 7:24; 8:14-19; 9:12-16
"A Rainbow And A Promise"

1. The Story

Reader: These are the descendants of Noah.
Noah was a righteous man, blameless in his
generation; Noah walked with God. And Noah had
three sons, Shem, Ham, and Japheth. Now the earth
was corrupt in God's sight, and the earth was filled
with violence. And God saw that the earth was
corrupt; for all flesh had corrupted its ways upon
the earth. And God said to Noah,

All: "I have determined to make an end of all
flesh, for the earth is filled with violence because of
them; now I am going to destroy them along with
the earth. Make yourself an ark of cypress wood;
make rooms in the ark, and cover it inside and
out with pitch. This is how you are to make it: the
length of the ark three hundred cubits, its width
fifty cubits, and its height thirty cubits. Make a roof
for the ark, and finish it to a cubit above; and put
the door of the ark in its side; make it with lower,
second, and third decks. For my part, I am going
to bring a flood of waters on the earth, to destroy
from under heaven all flesh in which is the breath
of life; everything that is on the earth shall die. But I
will establish my covenant with you; and you shall
come into the ark, you, your sons, your wife, and
your sons' wives with you. And of every living
thing, of all flesh, you shall bring two of every kind
into the ark, to keep them alive with you; they shall
be male and female. Of the birds according to their
kinds, and of the animals according to their kinds,
of every creeping thing of the ground according to
its kind, two of every kind shall come in to you, to
keep them alive. Also take with you every kind of

food that is eaten, and store it up; and it shall serve as food for you and for them."

Reader: Noah did this; he did all that God commanded him. And the waters swelled on the earth for one hundred fifty days. In the second month, on the twenty-seventh day of the month, the earth was dry. Then God said to Noah,

All: "Go out of the ark, you and your wife, and your sons and your sons' wives with you. Bring out with you every living thing that is with you of all flesh — birds and animals and every creeping thing that creeps on the earth — so that they may abound on the earth, and be fruitful and multiply on the earth."

Reader: So Noah went out with his sons and his wife and his sons' wives. And every animal, every creeping thing, and every bird, everything that moves on the earth, went out of the ark by families... God said,

All: "This is the sign of the covenant that I make between me and you and every living creature that is with you, for all future generations: I have set my bow in the clouds, and it shall be a sign of the covenant between me and the earth. When I bring clouds over the earth and the bow is seen in the clouds, I will remember my covenant that is between me and you and every living creature of all flesh; and the waters shall never again become a flood to destroy all flesh. When the bow is in the clouds, I will see it and remember the everlasting covenant between God and every living creature of all flesh that is on the earth."

Reader: Word of God, word of life.

All: Thanks be to God.

2. The Sermon

I found this story on the internet recently.

A year after the Lord told Noah to build the ark, the Lord saw that Noah was sitting in his front yard, weeping. And there was no ark. "Noah!" shouted the Lord, "Where is the ark?" "Lord, please forgive me!" begged Noah. "I did my best. But there were big problems. First, I had to get a building permit for the ark construction project, and your plans didn't meet code. I had to hire an engineer to redraw the plans. Then I got into a big fight over whether or not the ark needed a fire sprinkler system. "Then my neighbor objected, claiming I was violating zoning by building the ark in my front yard. I had to get a variance from the city planning commission. Then I had problems getting enough wood for the ark, because there was a ban on cutting trees to save the spotted owl. I had to convince the US Fish and Wildlife that I needed the wood to save the owls. But they wouldn't let me catch any owls. So, no owls. The carpenters formed a union and went out on strike. I had to negotiate a settlement with the National Labor Relations Board before anyone would pick up a saw or hammer. Now we have sixteen carpenters going on the boat, and still no owls. Then I started gathering up animals and got sued by an animal rights group. They objected to me taking only two of each kind. Just when I got that suit dismissed, the EPA notified me that I couldn't complete the ark without filing an environmental impact statement on your proposed flood. They didn't take kindly to the idea that they had no jurisdiction over the conduct of a supreme being. Then the Army Corps of Engineers wanted a map of the proposed new flood plain. So I sent them a globe. Right now, I'm still trying to resolve a complaint from the Equal

Employment Opportunity Commission over how many minorities I'm supposed to hire. The IRS has seized all my assets, claiming I'm trying to avoid paying taxes by leaving the country. And I just got a notice from the state about owing them some kind of use tax. I really don't think I can finish the ark for at least another five years," Noah wailed. The sky began to clear. The sun began to shine. A rainbow arched across the sky. Noah looked up and smiled, "You mean you're not going to destroy the earth?" Noah asked hopefully. "No," said the Lord sadly, "Government bureaucracy already has!"[8]

The story of Noah and the ark is a favorite for many. This story was the basis for a recent movie "Evan Almighty." Sadly, for many adults Noah's ark is just a kid's fairy tale, an unlikely and unbelievable story of animals on an ancient boat. What could it possibly mean for our modern and busy lives? If we focus on the difficulties in the story, on the animals, or on the dimensions of the boat, or on the waters covering the whole earth, we get sidetracked from the really important parts of the story, like what it has to say to us about God, or what it has to say to us about ourselves. Flood stories were common in the ancient world. What makes this one different? What did the author of this story say different that reveals something true about God?

Last Sunday we started this series with the creation story. In Genesis 1:31 God was exuberant over his new creation. God stepped back and looked with pride at the brand-new creation. **"God saw everything that he had made, and indeed, it was very good."** That feeling didn't last long. In just a few chapters we find one of the saddest verses in the Bible. **"The Lord saw that the wickedness of humankind was great in the earth, and that every inclination of the thoughts of their hearts was only evil continually. And the Lord was sorry that he had made humankind on the earth, and it grieved him to his heart"** (Genesis 6:5-6). God is profoundly sad and deeply grieved over the rebellion of his creation. So here is my question: What does

8 Author unknown.

26

it take to go from Genesis 1 to Genesis 6? What happens in the heart of God between the two? Why does God change from being incredibly proud to being sorry for creating the world in the first place?

When you think about it, is God really so different from any parent? When that baby is born they are so sweet and pure and innocent. We are incredibly proud and grateful for this amazing gift. But what happens when they child grows into their terrible twos and begin to explore their independence? Sometimes it is enough to make a parent want to tear their hair out.

Or is God any different from a new bride or bridegroom starting out life together so in love, full of hopes and dreams? The first year can be blissful. But after a while the personal habits and quirks of the other can start to irritate, and if couples don't know how to negotiate their way forward, they can end up miserable and wishing they had never gotten married.

Maybe that helps us to understand the reaction of God to an imperfect creation. God shows profound disappointment, sadness, grief and regret. And God's first impulse is to get rid of the old and start over again. And so, we have this story of flood waters covering the earth.

Have any of you experienced a flood? We've seen a lot of flooding locally and around the world recently. Wherever there's a flood, it can be devastating to the victims. When we see pictures of it on the news we recoil in horror. The story tells us that God, too, was sorry at the destruction. Perhaps even God recoiled in horror and promised to never destroy the world by a flood again. In chapter 8:21, "The Lord said in his heart, I will never again curse the ground because of humankind, for the inclination of the human heart is evil from youth; nor will I ever again destroy every living creature as I have done. As long as the earth endures, seedtime and harvest, cold and heat, summer and winter, day and night, shall not cease." The rainbow is a sign of that promise. One of the greatest insights from this story is that God changes. God interacts with the creation, God learns and God adapts. And so, one of the basic questions this story leads us to ask is — What is God like? What does this story teach us about God and who God is? How does God behave in the world?

27

Do you remember when the earthquake struck Haiti and there were some preachers who were saying that God was punishing them for a pact they had made with the devil 200 years earlier. Really? Does God behave that way? Or what about the AIDS epidemic and preachers suggesting that it was God's punishment for sin? When tragedy strikes in your life do you ever wonder if God is punishing you for some sin you committed? One of the lessons we learn from this Noah story is that this is not the way a loving God behaves. God is changed. In the end God is revealed as a promise maker and a promise keeper. God **"makes his sun rise on the evil and on the good and sends rain on the righteous and on the unrighteous"** (Matthew 5:45). God's goodness provides for the whole creation regardless of whether they behave or not. **"As long as the earth endures, seedtime and harvest, cold and heat, summer and winter, day and night, shall not cease."** God's faithfulness and love for the whole creation is reflected in the faithfulness of the seasons.

God doesn't have to punish us. We punish ourselves by our choices and our actions. We reap what we sow. But God does not just leave us to our tragic consequences. God does not resign himself to evil. God so loved the world that he gave his only begotten son. God came among us in Jesus. God doesn't threaten us with violence if we don't behave. What God learned through Noah is that you can't change the world through violence. It's love that changes people. God was in Christ, on the cross reconciling the world to himself. It's God's love that melts our selfish hearts and heals our brokenness. God changes the world through suffering, redemptive love in his Son, Jesus. God is coming to you today with love to create in you a new heart and mind, and God invites you to be a part of God's mission for the life of the world.

3. The Song — "Thy Holy Wings"

Proper 5 / Ordinary Time 10 — Genesis 12:1-9
"When God Calls"

1. The Story

Reader: Now the Lord said to Abram,

All: "Go from your country and your kindred and your father's house to the land that I will show you. I will make of you a great nation, and I will bless you, and make your name great, so that you will be a blessing. I will bless those who bless you, and the one who curses you I will curse; and in you all the families of the earth shall be blessed."

Reader: So Abram went, as the Lord had told him; and Lot went with him. Abram was 75 years old when he departed from Haran. Abram took his wife Sarai and his brother's son Lot, and all the possessions that they had gathered, and the persons whom they had acquired in Haran; and they set forth to go to the land of Canaan. When they had come to the land of Canaan, Abram passed through the land to the place at Shechem, to the oak of Moreh. At that time the Canaanites were in the land. Then the Lord appeared to Abram, and said,

All: "To your offspring I will give this land."

Reader: So he built there an altar to the Lord, who had appeared to him. From there he moved on to the hill country on the east of Bethel, and pitched his tent, with Bethel on the west and Ai on the east; and there he built an altar to the Lord and invoked the name of the Lord. And Abram journeyed on by stages toward the Negeb." Word of God, word of life.

All: Thanks be to God.

2. The Sermon

It was a little over two years ago that this congregation called me to come and be your pastor. That was a time of prayer and discernment for you as a congregation, and also for me and my family. Was God calling us to come to this place?

What does it mean to be called by God? How do we know when God is calling us somewhere? I suspect that many of you, too, have gone through a similar process when you have moved or made a major life decision, seeking God's will for your life, spending time in prayer and conversation with others, weighing together all the factors, positive and negative. I share this with you because I think it's a good way to begin thinking about our story today of the call given to Abraham and Sarah. They did not have the opportunity to check out ahead of time the place they were moving to. They just left home, with all their questions, trusting that God would provide for them.

This is one of the most important stories in the Old Testament. Scholars think it is the hinge on which the whole book of Genesis swings. It is a story that gives birth to three of our religions today — Christianity, Judaism and Islam. The story starts with the call of God. **"Now the LORD said to Abram, 'Go from your country and your kindred and your father's house to the land that I will show you.'"** Those of you who are married can imagine how you would feel if one day your spouse came to you announcing he or she had heard a voice from God that you should pack your bags and move. People who claim they hear voices are suspect. Add to that, Abraham and Sarah were told to leave home and all that was familiar, to move to a place they had never been before, unsure of what they would find when they got there. That takes a lot of courage and faith. Most of us want to have all the questions answered before we make a decision of that magnitude. That was certainly the case for me when I decided to move here. The story does not tell us whether Abraham and Sarah agonized over this decision or not. It simply says that they responded obediently. **"So Abram went, as the LORD had told him."** They trusted God and the promise God had given them. Hebrews 11 says this about Abraham and Sarah: **"By faith Abraham obeyed when he was called to set out for a place that he was to receive as an**

30

inheritance; and he set out, not knowing where he was going." No wonder Abraham is called the father of a nation. He trusted God to keep the promise. And his faith changed human history.

I love this story of Abraham and Sarah. Sometimes when we read the Bible we have a hard time seeing the people in its pages as real people. It's like Mother Teresa — we stand in awe of her but know in our hearts that we could never do what she did. The people of the Bible often get surrounded by so much "holy smoke" that we can't see that they are just as broken and flawed as we are. The Bible says that Abraham was 75 years old when God called him, and Sarah was 65, both well past their prime. And yet God called and used them. He didn't call someone young and beautiful. The story in Genesis 12 goes on to say that Abraham did some shameful things to save his own skin. He wasn't perfect, and yet God used him. At the end of the book of Joshua (24:2) it says this about Abraham. **"And Joshua said to all the people, "Thus says the LORD, the God of Israel: Long ago your ancestors — Terah and his sons Abraham and Nahor — lived beyond the Euphrates and served other gods."** In other words, God didn't choose Abraham and Sarah because they were all that good or worthy. In fact, when God called them they were serving other gods!

I love this story because I find that Abraham and Sarah are people just like you and me. We are imperfect people, broken and flawed by sin, people who spend too much of our time chasing after other gods. And yet God chooses to call and use imperfect people again and again. God has called us in the waters of baptism, called us to be his children, called us to follow his Son, Jesus Christ, and to trust God's promises to us. God calls us and sends us out into the world as imperfect people with a wonderful story to tell about a God who loves and forgives imperfect people and who keeps promises with them.

What is God's will for my life? Our high school graduates are asking that very question right now. I admire those that seem to have a sense of what they want to do. I think there are many more who really don't know yet. What is God's will for my life? Maybe you're at a point in your life where you are asking that same question. Maybe it's a decision about a move, or a relationship, or a career change. Sometimes God's will seems so obvious and we know exactly where we are headed and what God wants us to do. But then there are other times when we just aren't sure where we are going. We can't see the future; we don't have a clue. It's especially at those times that "we walk by faith and not by sight." We live the questions waiting for the answers. But as we walk, this much we do know. In the waters of baptism God made a covenant with us, a covenant God will never break. God has called us to believe in his Son, Jesus Christ, to trust in God's promise to "supply all our needs through his riches in Christ." And God has called us to go and share that good news with others. Maybe that will mean leaving home. For most of us though it will be a different kind of journey than leaving home. It may mean leaving all those safe and comfortable places to journey somewhere outside your comfort zone, a journey that Google Maps won't be able to show you. Maybe it's a journey you will take with a counselor to explore some of those issues that have been troubling you all your life. Maybe it's a journey to make new discoveries in a Bible study or a small group. Maybe it's a journey across the hall at school or work to share comforting words with someone who is hurting. It's a journey of faith, but as we go, we trust God's promises that it will be a journey filled with God's blessing.

One of my favorite prayers could well have been written by Abraham and Sarah. It is called the Prayer of Good Courage. May this be our prayer this week.

> "Lord God, you have called your servants to ventures of which we cannot see the ending, by paths as yet untrodden, through perils unknown. Give us faith to go out with good courage, not knowing where we go, but only that your hand is leading us and your love supporting us; through Jesus Christ our Lord. Amen."[9]

3. The Song — "Guide Me Ever, Great Redeemer"

9 Closing Prayer from the Vespers Service, *Lutheran Book of Worship* (Minneapolis, Augsburg Fortress Press, 1978.)

Proper 6 / Ordinary Time 11 — Genesis 18:1-15
"Is Anything Too Wonderful For The Lord"

1. The Story

Reader: The Lord appeared to Abraham by the oaks of Mamre, as he sat at the entrance of his tent in the heat of the day. He looked up and saw three men standing near him. When he saw them, he ran from the tent entrance to meet them, and bowed down to the ground. He said,

All: "My Lord, if I find favor with you, do not pass by your servant. Let a little water be brought, and wash your feet, and rest yourselves under the tree. Let me bring a little bread, that you may refresh yourselves, and after that you may pass on — since you have come to your servant."

Reader: So they said,

Pastor: "Do as you have said."

Reader: And Abraham hastened into the tent to Sarah, and said,

All: "Make ready quickly three measures of choice flour, knead it, and make cakes."

Reader: Abraham ran to the herd, and took a calf, tender and good, and gave it to the servant, who hastened to prepare it. Then he took curds and milk and the calf that he had prepared, and set it before them; and he stood by them under the tree while they ate. They said to him,

Pastor: "Where is your wife Sarah?"

All: "There, in the tent."

Pastor: "I will surely return to you in due season, and your wife Sarah shall have a son."

Reader: And Sarah was listening at the tent entrance behind him. Now Abraham and Sarah were old, advanced in age; it had ceased to be with Sarah after the manner of women. So Sarah laughed to herself, saying,

All: "After I have grown old, and my husband is old, shall I have pleasure?"

Reader: The Lord said to Abraham,

Pastor: "Why did Sarah laugh, and say, 'Shall I indeed bear a child, now that I am old?' Is anything too wonderful for the Lord? At the set time I will return to you, in due season, and Sarah shall have a son."

Reader: But Sarah denied, saying,

All: "I did not laugh,"

Reader: for she was afraid. He said,

Pastor: "Oh yes, you did laugh."

Reader: Word of God, word of life.

All: Thanks be to God.

2. The Sermon

Happy Father's Day to the dads out there. I remember becoming a father back in 1987 when my daughter was born. It was an emotional and overwhelming experience for me. I was overcome with gratitude, but also with some anxiety. This was new territory. Would I be a good father to this little child? I knew I would try my best. It's amazing how quickly our hearts get bonded to our children and we can't imagine life without them. I am amazed at the vast majority of good parents who pour their lives into their children. There are some parents who just seem to have a gift for parenting and it comes so easily for them, not just having children but raising them and teaching them.

A few weeks ago, we heard the creation story and God's charge to human beings to multiply and fill the earth, and to have dominion over the creation. We learned that having dominion means to bring order out of chaos, not to exploit for personal gain, but to care for and be good stewards of the earth. There are over seven billion people living on earth today. We are hard-wired to have children, to pass on our genes to the next generation. And while the vast majority of people choose to have children, some choose not to have children or choose to remain single. It amazes me how easily some couples get pregnant, and then how hard others try and fail. Many couples struggle with infertility. Some choose to adopt. Fortunately, today couples have many more options. Every child born is a miracle, but with modern medicine we have even more miracles.

It's appropriate on this Father's Day that we have this story about Abraham and Sarah. The name Abraham means "father of a nation." When God called Abraham and Sarah to leave their home and travel to a new land, God gave them a promise. God would give them land and many descendants, and through those descendants would come a blessing to the world. Abraham and Sarah left their home trusting in God's promise. Abraham was 75 and Sarah was 65 then, a time when most of us would rather just settle down and enjoy retirement. It's a similar story to that of my 3x Great Grandmother, Martha Synde. She was a widow in Norway and life was difficult. In 1850, at the age of 65, she moved almost her entire family, 28 people, across the ocean in a sailing ship to settle in Southern Wisconsin. I can't imagine the hardships they went through. Now think about Abraham and Sarah, some 3,500 years ago, making a similar move, trusting in God's promise to them. But 25 years later, after Sarah had gone through menopause, they were still childless. You must understand that at that time, a woman's value was seen in her ability to produce children. If she had many children, she was blessed by God. If she was barren, she was cursed by God. Abraham and Sarah had trusted God, but in their old age were tempted to lose faith in the promise. In fact, they came up with a plan to help God. Abraham would have children through Sarah's handmaiden, Hagar.

35

That's the situation when our story takes place. Abraham was 100 and Sarah was 90. I imagine that they had little hope anymore that a child would be born to them. So, when visitors showed up and announced that Sarah was going to bear a son, they were met with laughter. It wasn't the laughter of joy; it was the scoffing laugh of a sceptic.

I was 32 and 34 years old when my children were born. Many of you had your children in your twenties. There's a reason we have children when we are young. They take a lot of energy. I can't imagine what it would be like to have a child in old age. My parents were 47 and 41 when my twin sister and I were born. They were old enough to be our grandparents. My parents did the best they could. It was good they had my older brothers and sisters to help out. But can you imagine having a child when you were ninety years old?

This last week I googled "oldest woman to give birth" and found an interesting article. There is a fertility clinic in India that treated a woman who gave birth to a child at the age of 72. The father was 79. The mother said this: "I feel blessed to be able to hold my own baby. I had lost hope of ever becoming a mother ever.... Everyone asked me to adopt a baby, but I never wanted to. I had faith in almighty, and knew I will bear my child one day." Amazingly, the child was born healthy. There is a striking picture of the proud couple holding their new baby.[10] You can see the joy and the pride in their faces. Something they had longed and hoped for their whole lives was finally fulfilled. While you and I might never want a child in our old age, it sure is great to have grandchildren to spoil, and then send them home.

There's an interesting phrase in the story. Sarah laughed when she heard the news about getting pregnant. **"The Lord said to Abraham, 'Why did Sarah laugh, and say, "Shall I indeed bear a child, now that I am old?" Is anything too wonderful for the Lord?'"** It's a great question and one that I hope you take home and ponder throughout this next week. Is anything too wonderful for the Lord? Say it with me. If I had asked the question, I would

10 Jack Philips, "Oldest Mother in the World: Meet the Woman Who Had Her First Child in Her 70s," August 29, 2019, https://www.theepochtimes.com/oldest-mother-in-the-world-meet-the-woman-who-had-her-first-child-in-her-70s_3061687.html, (accessed August 13, 2020).

have said, "Is anything too impossible for the Lord? Is anything too difficult for the Lord?" But no, the question is, is anything too wonderful for the Lord? We serve a God who is not only powerful, but a God who loves us and wants the best for us, a God who wants to give us the desires of our hearts. Those desires may not be completely fulfilled in this life, but they certainly will be in the life to come.

There is an echo of this story in the New Testament. Do you remember when the angel came to Mary and told her that she would bear a son? The angel also told her about another special birth. **"And now, your relative Elizabeth in her old age has also conceived a son; and this is the sixth month for her who was said to be barren. For nothing will be impossible with God."** Did you catch it? Nothing will be impossible with God. Is anything too wonderful for the Lord?

There may be situations you are facing where you are tempted to give up, tempted to despair, tempted to doubt and give up on life. Just remember that we belong to a God who specializes in hopeless cases. We belong to a God who can give a child to an elderly barren couple. We belong to a God who can heal the sick. And we belong to a God who can raise the dead. Talk about a hopeless case. In Jesus Christ, God turned death into resurrection and changed everything. Our sins are forgiven, and we are made new.

When God called Abraham and Sarah, God promised them three things — land, descendants, and that through those descendants a blessing would come to the world. God kept his promise and gave us his Son, Jesus, a descendant of Abraham. And the world has been blessed through him. Is anything too wonderful for the Lord? In Jesus Christ, the answer is "No! Nothing will be impossible with God."

3. The Song — "Blessed Be The God Of Israel"

Proper 7 / Ordinary Time 12 — Genesis 21:8-21
"God Hears Our Cries"

1. The Story

Reader: The child grew and was weaned; and Abraham made a great feast on the day that Isaac was weaned. But Sarah saw the son of Hagar the Egyptian, whom she had borne to Abraham, playing with her son Isaac. So she said to Abraham,

All: "Cast out this slave woman with her son; for the son of this slave woman shall not inherit along with my son Isaac."

Reader: The matter was very distressing to Abraham on account of his son. But God said to Abraham,

Pastor: "Do not be distressed because of the boy and because of your slave woman; whatever Sarah says to you, do as she tells you, for it is through Isaac that offspring shall be named for you. As for the son of the slave woman, I will make a nation of him also, because he is your offspring."

Reader: So Abraham rose early in the morning, and took bread and a skin of water, and gave it to Hagar, putting it on her shoulder, along with the child, and sent her away. And she departed and wandered about in the wilderness of Beersheba. When the water in the skin was gone, she cast the child under one of the bushes. Then she went and sat down opposite him a good way off, about the distance of a bowshot; for she said,

All: "Do not let me look on the death of the child."

Reader: And as she sat opposite him, she lifted up her voice and wept. And God heard the voice of the boy; and the angel of God called to Hagar from heaven, and said to her,

Pastor: "What troubles you, Hagar? Do not be afraid; for God has heard the voice of the boy where he is. Come, lift up the boy and hold him fast with your hand, for I will make a great nation of him."

Reader: Then God opened her eyes and she saw a well of water. She went, and filled the skin with water, and gave the boy a drink. God was with the boy, and he grew up; he lived in the wilderness, and became an expert with the bow. He lived in the wilderness of Paran; and his mother got a wife for him from the land of Egypt." Word of God, word of life.

All: Thanks be to God.

2. The Sermon

One of the things many families plan in the summer is a family reunion. We had a reunion in my wife's family last summer up in Fargo, and we combined it with a celebration of her father's ninetieth birthday. Now that he has had a stroke, we are glad we did that while he still had good health. On my family's side, we tend to have a big reunion about every five years. Our last family reunion was in 2013 and we met at Luther College in Decorah, Iowa. Generally, I look forward to family reunions. It's good to catch up with cousins I haven't seen in many years. But there are a few family members that are more, shall we say, challenging. They require extra grace. Do you know what I mean? Do you have anyone like that in your family? One branch of my family seems to bear emotional scars from their upbringing, and I feel like every time we get together we have to engage in some sort of group therapy with them. Oh well. Families come in all shapes and flavors. Some are healthy, but most share some level of dysfunction.

Today we are talking about Abraham and Sarah's family. It is full of dysfunction and pain. You'd expect for a family to appear in the Bible that it would be white washed and all prettied up to make it look good. But the author of Genesis didn't do that. He pictures them as flawed and broken people who made a mess of their lives and those around them.

Last week we heard the story of Abraham and Sarah in their old age finally being blessed with a child that God had promised them. It was a joyous time filled with laughter. But scratch below the surface and you find a different story. It wasn't all "sweetness and light." Before Isaac was born, and after years of trying, Abraham and Sarah grew tired of waiting for the child God had promised them. So, they came up with a plan to help God. Sarah gave Abraham her handmaid, Hagar, to have children with. Ishmael was born, but so were all kinds of family tensions. There was jealousy and infighting among Sarah and Hagar. And then when Isaac was born, there was tension between Ishmael and Isaac. Things came to a head when Sarah told Abraham that Hagar and her son Ishmael must go. So, Abraham sent them out into the desert where they almost died of thirst. But God heard their cry.

The name Ishmael means "God hears." God heard the pain in this broken family. God heard the cry of a desperate mother. God heard the fear in young Ishmael as he left the only home he had ever known. God heard and God provided for them. The real hero in this story is God who has particularly good hearing.

- God heard the cries of the Israelites when they were enslaved in Egypt.
- God heard the cries of his people in the book of Judges and sent them deliverers again and again.
- God heard the cries of Mary and Martha as they grieved the death of their brother Lazarus.
- God heard the cries of a world in need of a Savior and God loved that world so much he sent his only Son. Through Jesus' death and resurrection, we learn the power of love and forgiveness to change our hearts and our world.

Ishmael and Isaac are still fighting with each other. The Bible tells us that the descendants of Ishmael became the Arab nations.

The descendants of Ishmael and the descendants of Isaac are half-brothers, but they can't seem to get along and stop fighting with each other. And the world is paying a terrible price in a legacy of pain and violence. It's as contemporary as the evening news with the president's son-in-law going to Israel to try to broker a peace deal between the Israelis and the Palestinians. We must pray for peace because this conflict is the root of much conflict in our world today.

God made a covenant with Abraham and Sarah. Isaac was the son chosen to carry that promise. But the interesting twist in this story is that God also made a covenant with Hagar and Ishmael. God didn't choose one and reject the other. God chose them both. God loved them both and provided for them both and made promises to them both. And if the promise to Isaac is still good today, so is the promise to Ishmael. The answer for us today is not to kill the enemy and wipe them off the face of the earth. The answer is to learn to love our enemy, to turn an enemy into a friend. This is what we learn from our Lord Jesus who met violence with love and forgiveness. This is what it means to be a Christian, a follower of Jesus Christ.

Do you like this story of Hagar and Ishmael? I do. It tells me that God loves imperfect people and imperfect families. God isn't afraid to get into the mess we make of our lives and bring his love and forgiveness. God doesn't tell us to clean up our act before we are good enough for God to hear our prayers. I know some people who wouldn't dare step inside a church. That's for the "good people." They feel that they could never measure up. But that is not the kind of God we see in this story. No, God hears the prayers of flawed and broken people and enters into their lives to bring blessing. God is here today in his son Jesus to bless you with his love. He is here in the bread and wine of Holy Communion to give you the assurance that God is with you, your sins are forgiven. Just like Isaac and Ishmael, God has made a covenant with you in the waters of baptism. You are part of God's family.

If you have a family reunion this summer, I hope you remember this story and the love God has for everyone, even those who require extra grace. You know, Abraham is really the father of three great religions — Judaism, Christianity and Islam. We may not be brothers and sisters to our Jewish and Muslim neighbors, but we are cousins, part of the same great big family. Let's learn to love each other.

3. The Song – "Out Of The Depths I Cry To You"

Proper 8 / Ordinary Time 13 — Genesis 22:1-14
"Making Deals With God"

1. The Story

Reader: After these things God tested Abraham. He said to him,

Pastor: "Abraham!"

All: "Here I am."

Pastor: "Take your son, your only son Isaac, whom you love, and go to the land of Moriah, and offer him there as a burnt offering on one of the mountains that I shall show you."

Reader: So Abraham rose early in the morning, saddled his donkey, and took two of his young men with him, and his son Isaac; he cut the wood for the burnt offering, and set out and went to the place in the distance that God had shown him. On the third day Abraham looked up and saw the place far away. Then Abraham said to his young men,

All: "Stay here with the donkey; the boy and I will go over there; we will worship, and then we will come back to you."

Reader: Abraham took the wood of the burnt offering and laid it on his son Isaac, and he himself carried the fire and the knife. So the two of them walked on together. Isaac said to his father Abraham,

Second Reader: "Father!"

All: "Here I am, my son."

Second Reader: "The fire and the wood are here, but where is the lamb for a burnt offering?"

All: "God himself will provide the lamb for a burnt offering, my son."

Reader: So the two of them walked on together. When they came to the place that God had shown him, Abraham built an altar there and laid the wood in order. He bound his son Isaac, and laid him on the altar, on top of the wood. Then Abraham reached out his hand and took the knife to kill his son. But the angel of the Lord called to him from heaven, and said,

Pastor: "Abraham, Abraham!"

All: "Here I am."

Pastor: "Do not lay your hand on the boy or do anything to him; for now I know that you fear God, since you have not withheld your son, your only son, from me."

Reader: And Abraham looked up and saw a ram, caught in a thicket by its horns. Abraham went and took the ram and offered it up as a burnt offering instead of his son. So Abraham called that place "The Lord will provide"; as it is said to this day, "On the mount of the Lord it shall be provided." Here ends the reading.

2. The Sermon

Almost a year ago a story appeared in the news of a father in New Orleans who killed his daughter because "God told him to." The man told police that "God made him do it," and described to them how he had stabbed and suffocated her. After killing his daughter, the man called the police to tell them to come and arrest him. This kind of story appears in the news every so often and it horrifies those of us who are parents. A normal parent could not even begin to imagine harming a child. In our effort to understand this kind of behavior, we often label it mental illness.

And our underlying assumption is that no god worthy of worship would ever ask a parent to do something like that.

But that is precisely what we have in our story today. God commanded Abraham to take his son, the son of the promise, the one he had waited so long for, and sacrifice him as an offering to God. I have to admit that I am terrified of this story. I don't like it. I wish it weren't in the Bible. What kind of god would do this? Certainly not the God I worship in Jesus Christ. So why is this story here and why do we have to tell it?

It is a fair question that deserves a thoughtful answer. Child sacrifice was common in ancient Israel and surrounding countries. Archaeologists have discovered the bones of small children in the foundation of homes. It is a horrifying way of making a deal with god. "God, if I give up something most precious to me, then I am demonstrating my commitment to you. I'm trying to get your attention with this extravagant gift. I want you to bless me. I want you to prosper me and bring me success." We modern people shudder at the thought that child sacrifice would ever be required or acceptable to God. But I wonder if the underlying assumption of bartering with God or making deals with God isn't still alive and well in our hearts today?

I wonder if some of us don't see God like a divine candy machine. You put the proper coins in, press the right button and out comes the candy you want. The real question this kind of religion is asking is this: how do we get God to do the things we want God to do for us? Is there a way we can manipulate God so that God will bless us?

Sometimes I wonder if much of our religion today isn't like that — a series of bargains we make with God so that God will bless us. Have you ever given up something for Lent that you really enjoyed, like chocolate, for example? I sometimes wonder if we don't treat that like a transaction with God. God if I give this up, will you do something for me? If I pray really hard, if I promise to go to church every Sunday, if I... (you fill in the blank), will you bless me?

The underlying assumption with that kind of religion is that we can manipulate God, that we can make deals with God. That

45

was the kind of environment Abraham lived in. And so, when he heard the voice in his head telling him to sacrifice his son, Abraham didn't flinch. The end result was that God sent an angel to stop Abraham, to tell him not to sacrifice his son. Many scholars feel that this story is precisely here to say that child sacrifice was not necessary, and that God does not require it or even approve of it.

The reality is that we can't manipulate God to do what we want. We can only submit to God. In the Abraham story, God came to Abraham and Sarah. God made a covenant with them. That was an act of grace. They didn't manipulate God, they only submitted to God in faith. Later, with Moses, we will learn in the Ten Commandments how God wants us to behave. We don't obey the commandments in order to get God to love us. God already loves us. We obey the commandments in response to God's love for us. And when we do that, there will be blessings.

As I said earlier, I don't like this story. It is terrifying. But even here in this frightening story, there is a word of grace. As Abraham and Isaac walked up the mountain to make a sacrifice, Isaac asked his father where the lamb was for the offering. And Abraham replied that God himself would provide the lamb. And God did provide the sacrifice. There in the thicket was a ram, caught by its horns. That was what Abraham sacrificed. He didn't bring God something that was valuable to sacrifice to God. God provided the sacrifice.

That is exactly what God has done for us in Jesus Christ. Jesus is the Lamb of God who takes away the sins of the world. God has provided his own Son for our forgiveness. Our sins are forgiven. That is the good news we celebrate today.

We don't make deals with God. We only respond out of faith and love for all that God has given us. We love because God has first loved us in his Son, Jesus Christ. Amen.

3. The Song — "My Hope Is Built On Nothing Less"; "Rock Of Ages"

Proper 9 / Ordinary Time 14 — Genesis 24:34-38, 42-49, 58-67
"Matchmaker, Matchmaker"

1. The Story

Reader: So he said, "I am Abraham's servant. The Lord has greatly blessed my master, and he has become wealthy; he has given him flocks and herds, silver and gold, male and female slaves, camels and donkeys. And Sarah my master's wife bore a son to my master when she was old; and he has given him all that he has. My master made me swear, saying, 'You shall not take a wife for my son from the daughters of the Canaanites, in whose land I live; but you shall go to my father's house, to my kindred, and get a wife for my son.' "I came today to the spring, and said, 'O Lord, the God of my master Abraham, if now you will only make successful the way I am going! I am standing here by the spring of water; let the young woman who comes out to draw, to whom I shall say, "Please give me a little water from your jar to drink," and who will say to me, "Drink, and I will draw for your camels also" — let her be the woman whom the Lord has appointed for my master's son.' "Before I had finished speaking in my heart, there was Rebekah coming out with her water jar on her shoulder; and she went down to the spring, and drew. I said to her, 'Please let me drink.' She quickly let down her jar from her shoulder, and said, 'Drink, and I will also water your camels.' So I drank, and she also watered the camels. Then I asked her, 'Whose daughter are you?' She said, 'The daughter of Bethuel, Nahor's son, whom Milcah bore to him.' So I put the ring on her nose and the bracelets on her arms. Then I bowed my head and worshiped the Lord, and blessed the Lord, the God of my master Abraham, who had led me by the right way to obtain the daughter of my master's kinsman for his son. Now then, if you will deal loyally and truly with my master, tell me; and if not, tell me, so that I may turn either to the right hand or to the left." And they called Rebekah, and said to her,

Men: "Will you go with this man?"

Women: "I will."

Reader: So they sent away their sister Rebekah and her nurse along with Abraham's servant and his men. And they blessed Rebekah and said to her,

All: "May you, our sister, become thousands of myriads; may your offspring gain possession of the gates of their foes."

Reader: Then Rebekah and her maids rose up, mounted the camels, and followed the man; thus the servant took Rebekah, and went his way. Now Isaac had come from Beer-lahai-roi, and was settled in the Negeb. Isaac went out in the evening to walk in the field; and looking up, he saw camels coming. And Rebekah looked up, and when she saw Isaac, she slipped quickly from the camel, and said to the servant,

Women: "Who is the man over there, walking in the field to meet us?"

Reader: The servant said, "It is my master." So she took her veil and covered herself. And the servant told Isaac all the things that he had done. Then Isaac brought her into his mother Sarah's tent. He took Rebekah, and she became his wife; and he loved her. So Isaac was comforted after his mother's death." Word of God, word of life.

All: Thanks be to God.

2. The Sermon

It's a tale as old as time. Boy meets girl; girl meets boy. There is an attraction. They fall in love and live happily ever after. At least that's the modern fantasy. But for most of human history, it hasn't happened that way. Even in some cultures today, marriages are still arranged. The choice of a marriage partner is not made by young, inexperienced people with raging hormones. It is often made by parents who have other considerations in mind. In an arranged marriage, you get to know your spouse after the wedding. Love for your partner grows over time.

It reminds me of a scene in the musical, *Fiddler on the Roof*. Tevye asks his wife, Golde, a question. "Do you love me?" She replied, "Do I love you? For twenty-five years, I've washed your clothes, cooked your meals, cleaned your house, given you children, milked your cow — after twenty-five years, why talk about love right now?" Tevje replied, "Golde, the first time I met you was on our wedding day. I was scared... I was nervous... But my father and my mother said we'd learn to love each other. And now I'm asking, Golde, do you love me?" Golde becomes a little thoughtful. "Do I love him? For twenty-five years I've lived with him, fought with him, starved with him, twenty-five years my bed is his, if that's not love, what is?" Tevye exclaims, "Then you love me?" Golde replies, "I suppose I do." And Tevje responds, "And I suppose I love you too."[11] Tevje and Golde had an arranged marriage that worked for them.

An arranged marriage is what we see in our story today. Abraham's most trusted servant found a suitable wife for Abraham's son Isaac. Rebekah just happened to be in the right place at the right time. She was willing to leave home and family, travel to a foreign land and marry a man she had never met. And somehow through it all, God was at work. There is a touching end to the story. It says that Isaac brought Rebekah **"into his mother Sarah's tent. He took Rebekah, and she became his wife; and he loved her"** (Genesis 24:67). Just like Tevje and Golde, they learned to love each other.

---

11 Jewison, N. (producer/director), 1971. *Fiddler on the Roof* [motion picture] United States: United Artists.

We all enjoy a good love story. When I meet with couples to plan their wedding, one of the first questions I ask them is how they met. It's always fun to listen to couples share their story. It happens in lots of ways. Sometimes they've known each other for years and are childhood sweethearts. Sometimes they meet in college. Sometimes they are introduced through a mutual friend. What's becoming more common is the number of couples who meet online.

Dr. Neil Clark Warren is the founder and director of one of the most popular relationship websites today, eHarmony, which claims that 66 million people have used eHarmony. In 2012 it was responsible for 160,000 marriages in the US. eHarmony is based on scientific research which claims that lasting marriages are based on couples sharing core compatibilities. eHarmony researchers say that the single factor that most likely makes a relationship work over the long haul is having core similarities. Many of you have heard that old saying about opposites attracting. What eHarmony claims is that healthy, satisfying, lasting marriages are based on shared core similarities. Instead of parents making a match for you, a computer finds you a compatible match.

In our Genesis story, Abraham was 140 years old and worried that his forty-year-old son wasn't married yet. If God's promise was going to be fulfilled, Isaac would need to find a wife and start a family. Abraham was too old to travel, so he charged his most trusted servant with the task. The only instruction Abraham gave him was that Isaac's wife must not be a Canaanite woman.

Some of you are old enough to remember a time when Lutherans were warned not to date Catholics or Catholics not to date Lutherans. Thankfully, times have changed, and we're just happy if our kids go to any church. I think Abraham is demonstrating common wisdom that a lasting relationship needs to be built on spiritual compatibility. Canaanite women worship different gods. How can Isaac be faithful to his God if his wife is always pulling him in a different direction? The New Testament says something similar in 2 Corinthians 6:14, **"Do not be mismatched with unbelievers."** Literally it says don't be unequally yoked with unbelievers. A yoke is a curved wooden bar that fits across the necks of two animals used to pull a plow or wagon. And if you yoke together a short ox and tall ox, or a fast horse and a slow horse, you're asking for trouble. And this is especially true when it comes to spiritual compatibility in marriage. If you and your partner aren't pulling in the same direction, it could cause you some heartache over the years.

As the story unfolds, Abraham's servant must find the right wife for Isaac. How is he going to decide? What does he look for? Should he advertise in the local paper? Should he hold a beauty or talent contest? The clever servant showed up at the well when women of the village went to draw water. He developed a test. He would ask a woman for a drink of water and if she offered to draw water for his camels as well, she would be the one. What was this servant looking for in a woman? He was looking for someone who had compassion and hospitality, a sensitivity to the needs of others. To draw water for a man was one thing but to draw enough water from a deep well for a thirsty camel was a lot of hard work. By making that generous offer a woman was showing that she was a hard worker and kind-hearted. This servant found all of those qualities in Rebekah.

There was something else Abraham told his trusted servant. Genesis 24:7 says, **"The LORD, the God of heaven, who... spoke to me and swore to me, 'To your offspring I will give this land,' he will send his angel before you, and you shall take a wife for my son from there."** Abraham had already had several encounters with angels. Abraham trusted that the same God would be with his servant and bless his journey to find a wife for Isaac. But this story is different. There are no angels, no dreams or visions, no voices from heaven. In this story, what we have are simple people of faith, who surround their lives with prayer and trust that God will guide them. And what we learn is that God was with them, though often acting in hidden ways, through ordinary events and circumstances. Isn't that often the way it is for us today? We may wonder where God is. We may ask for a special sign or want to know the will of God. We don't hear a voice from heaven, but God is there quietly working in the background. Sometimes the only way we can sense God's presence is to look back over the events of our lives and realize that God was there, all along the way, providing in quiet ways through the circumstances of life.

God is here today, in very ordinary and unremarkable circumstances. God is here in ordinary bread and wine. God is here in ordinary spoken words by an ordinary pastor. God often works in quiet unremarkable ways to bless us and provide us with daily bread.

Some of us choose to marry and be yoked to another person in life. Some of us choose not to marry. But all of us are invited to do life yoked together with Jesus. In our Gospel reading today, Jesus said, "Take my yoke upon you, for my yoke is easy, and my burden is light." Life is often a challenge. Isn't it good to know we have someone who wants to share that burden with us, someone who loves us to the point of giving his life for us? Whether we are single or married, let's do life together with Jesus.

3. The Song — "Blest Be The Tie That Binds"

Proper 10 / Ordinary Time 15 — Genesis 25:19-34
"The Trouble With Twins"

1. The Story

Reader: "These are the descendants of Isaac, Abraham's son: Abraham was the father of Isaac, and Isaac was forty years old when he married Rebekah, daughter of Bethuel the Aramean of Paddan-aram, sister of Laban the Aramean. Isaac prayed to the Lord for his wife, because she was barren; and the Lord granted his prayer, and his wife Rebekah conceived. The children struggled together within her; and she said,

Women: "If it is to be this way, why do I live?"

Reader: So she went to inquire of the Lord. And the Lord said to her,

Pastor: "Two nations are in your womb, and two peoples born of you shall be divided; the one shall be stronger than the other, the elder shall serve the younger."

Reader: When her time to give birth was at hand, there were twins in her womb. The first came out red, all his body like a hairy mantle; so they named him Esau. Afterward his brother came out, with his hand gripping Esau's heel; so he was named Jacob. Isaac was sixty years old when she bore them. When the boys grew up, Esau was a skillful hunter, a man of the field, while Jacob was a quiet man, living in tents. Isaac loved Esau, because he was fond of game; but Rebekah loved Jacob. Once when Jacob was cooking a stew, Esau came in from the field, and he was famished. Esau said to Jacob,

Pastor: "Let me eat some of that red stuff, for I am famished!"

Reader: (Therefore he was called Edom.) Jacob said,

All: "First sell me your birthright."

Pastor: "I am about to die; of what use is a birthright to me?"

All: "Swear to me first."

Reader: So he swore to him, and sold his birthright to Jacob. Then Jacob gave Esau bread and lentil stew, and he ate and drank, and rose and went his way. Thus Esau despised his birthright." Word of God, word of life.

All: Thanks be to God.

2. The Sermon

I'm wondering if we have anyone here today who is a twin? I learned something about twins. From 1915 to 1980 the percentage of twins born was 2% of all births. From 1980 to 1995 the percentage was 2.5%. After 2001, the rate surpassed 3%, and today one out of every thirty babies born is a twin. I had no idea. I wonder why that birth rate is increasing.

People who don't know me well are often surprised to learn that I have a twin sister. The story goes that my parents didn't know they were having twins. My mother claimed she had an inkling that she was bigger than usual. This was her fifth pregnancy. Both my parents were older. Mom was 41 and Dad was 47. Can you imagine having twins at that age? Uff da! I think they were in denial. Anyway, the first my father knew about it was when he was in the waiting room and the doctor came in and asked him, "Are you the man whose wife is having twins?" I think Dad must have fainted. My twin sister was born first, eight minutes before me, a fact that she never lets me forget. I tell her that I was just being polite. You know — ladies first. There are twins who talk about having a special bond with each other.

I'm not sure why my parents chose the names they did for us, other than they wanted two Norwegian names that started with the same letter. In many cultures, a name reflects the person. For example, do you remember when the movie, *Dances with Wolves*, came out? The name was given the main character because the Indians saw him dancing with wolves one day. In fact, in the Native American culture back then, a name wasn't given until a child was older. The parents observed the personality of the child and gave them a name that was appropriate. Names function differently in our culture. Most of us don't even know what our name means. It's not important. It's just a name. I learned that the name Rolf is a shortened form of Rudolph, and that it means "cunning" or "advised by wolves." I don't dance with wolves, but I guess I listen to them. Do you know what your name means?

In our Bible story from Genesis we have the birth of a set of twins, Esau and Jacob. The name "Esau" means rough and hairy, and it says that is what he was. Jacob came out second grabbing his brother's heel. That's what the name Jacob means, a heel-grabber, a trickster, a deceiver. Apparently, even in the womb these two were fighting with each other to the point that their mother, Rebekah, almost wanted to die. It became a symbol of their adult relationship. Esau, the firstborn, was red and hairy. He's the strong one, a skillful hunter, a real man's man. And then there's Jacob. He's described as being quiet, someone who spent more time at home than out in the field. He was a real "Momma's boy." Two sons born at the same time could not be more different than night and day.

The story tells us something else. It says that Isaac loved Esau, and Rebekah loved Jacob. Why is this important for us to know? How many of you have children? How many of you have more than one child? It is amazing how different they can be! As parents, we know how important it is to treat each child equally to avoid problems. Kids can sense if they're not being treated fairly. We are all human, however, and sometimes it's hard not to develop favorites. When parents have favorites, it can lead to all kinds of problems. And that is exactly what happened in this story.

Jacob and Esau fought with each other. Esau was bigger and stronger and picked on his brother. Jacob went crying to his mother and she whispered in his ear, "Don't worry my clever little heel-grabber. Let me show you how to handle your brother. We have ways to turn this around so that the older will serve the younger."

Does this sound familiar at all? Have any of you experienced sibling rivalry in your family? It can be really distressing when siblings fight. But how wonderful when they get along! Psalm 133:1 says, "Behold, how good and pleasant it is when brothers dwell in unity!" (RSV).

There's one more story about these two twin brothers. Esau came in from a frustrating hunting trip. He had gotten nothing. He was starving and not making the best decisions. And Jacob offered him a bowl of stew if his brother would give him his birthright. Remember, as the oldest, Esau stood to inherit twice as much as Jacob. He would also be the leader of the family. Jacob wanted the birthright for himself and he manipulated Esau in a weak moment with a bowl of stew. The fact that Esau was willing to give all that up for a bowl of stew doesn't make him look too good.

We haven't heard the last of these twins. It's not surprising that Jacob and Esau's relationship got much worse. It truly was a dysfunctional family. But I find something comforting in that. As I learn more about my own family and ancestors, there are plenty of stories that I'm not proud of. Every family has their black sheep, skeletons in the family closet. If God can love Jacob and Esau and even use them, then God can certainly love us and use us. God doesn't abandon us just because we aren't perfect.

The Bible gives us a realistic picture of real and imperfect people. They don't look and act much like heroes of the faith. And I suppose the point is that they aren't heroes. The real hero in this story is God. These stories in Genesis are really about a loving God, who chooses to be in relationship with weak and flawed human beings. And these stories will ultimately point us to a God, who sends his only Son to die for us so that we could have new life.

Jacob heel-grabber was no hero of the faith, no role model for us to emulate. He was a liar and deceiver. Next week we are going to hear a story of how the trickster himself got tricked. Some people call it, *karma*. Jacob did nothing to deserve God's blessing, yet God blessed him anyway. It was a gift of grace because God loved Jacob. We learn the same thing in Jesus Christ, that God so loved the world. We have done nothing to deserve that love, but God has given it to us in his Son. That is what we celebrate today. You are loved! You are forgiven. Share that love with others, even those that are hard to love.

3. The Song — "We Are Called"

Proper 11 / Ordinary Time 16 — Genesis 28:10-19a
"God Is Climbing Jacob's Ladder"

1. The Story

Reader: Jacob left Beer-sheba and went toward Haran. He came to a certain place and stayed there for the night, because the sun had set. Taking one of the stones of the place, he put it under his head and lay down in that place. And he dreamed that there was a ladder set up on the earth, the top of it reaching to heaven; and the angels of God were ascending and descending on it. And the Lord stood beside him and said,

Pastor: "I am the Lord, the God of Abraham your father and the God of Isaac; the land on which you lie I will give to you and to your offspring; and your offspring shall be like the dust of the earth, and you shall spread abroad to the west and to the east and to the north and to the south; and all the families of the earth shall be blessed in you and in your offspring. Know that I am with you and will keep you wherever you go, and will bring you back to this land; for I will not leave you until I have done what I have promised you."

Reader: Then Jacob woke from his sleep and said,

All: "Surely the Lord is in this place — and I did not know it!"

Reader: And he was afraid, and said,

All: "How awesome is this place! This is none other than the house of God, and this is the gate of heaven."

Reader: So Jacob rose early in the morning, and he took the stone that he had put under his head and set it up for a pillar and poured oil on the top of it. He called that place Bethel..." Word of God, word of life.

All: Thanks be to God.

2. The Sermon

How many of you grew up singing that spiritual, "We are Climbing Jacob's Ladder"?

1. We are climbing Jacob's ladder (3x) Soldiers of the Cross.
2. Ev'ry rung goes higher, higher (3x) Soldiers of the Cross.

I loved singing that song as a young boy. I knew what a ladder was and how to climb it. And somehow in my young brain, I got the idea that the higher I climbed that ladder the closer I got to God. God was up and I was down. My goal in life was to get up that ladder as high as I could. I did that by following the rules and doing good things for others. To me, that's what it meant to be a good Christian — obey the commandments and love others.

I think that in the minds of many people this is the essence of religion. If you believe in a higher power, then how do you get that higher power to hear your prayers? How do you get that higher power to love you? Well, you do what that higher power wants you to do.

Let me give you an example. When I was in high school, I had a girlfriend who was Mormon. I learned a lot about the Mormon church from her. For instance, I learned that they believe that God was once a human being. As a human, God climbed the ladder, became divine and populated our world with God's own spirit children. I learned that in the Mormon theology Jesus is just a little farther down the ladder. I also learned that if human beings climbed the ladder, they too someday could become gods and have their own worlds to watch over and populate it with their own spirit children.

Now don't get me wrong. I love Mormon people. As far as good, kind, moral, and ethical people are concerned, there are none better. There is a lot I respect about the Mormon church, too. But when it comes to their beliefs about God, not so much. When you dig deep enough into Mormon religion, their god is vastly different than anything traditional Christianity has ever

59

taught. The reason I bring this up, however, is that the Mormon religion is Jacob's ladder on steroids. You earn your way into the top level of heaven by your good deeds. And God rewards your good deeds by promoting you.

Now I want you to keep all that in mind as we explore this story from Genesis, chapter 28. The main character is Jacob, a fine upstanding young man, of exemplary character, respectful of his parents, and everyone loves him. Right? Wrong! What we have in this story is a young man who was a liar and a cheat, who schemed with his mother to deceive his father and defraud his older brother. His brother was angry enough to kill, and Jacob had to run for his life. Now, these are not the kind of conservative family values that we would want to promote. If we were to judge Jacob on the standard of the Ten Commandments, he would fail miserably. Jacob had no moral center. He was a liar, a cheat and a thief, willing to do anything to gain power and wealth. I imagine that for him, God was largely irrelevant to his everyday life. He'd heard the old stories that his parents had told him about God and God's promise to them. As far as Jacob was concerned, they were silly old myths. Religion is for children and the weak. Jacob knew better. You have to look out for yourself because no one else will. You do whatever you have to do in order to get ahead. But now Jacob's scheming had finally gotten him into real trouble. As he fled for his life, do you suppose he felt some remorse? He was alone, vulnerable, without friends or family to protect him. Finally, exhausted, he lay down with nothing but a rock for a pillow and fell asleep. This was no Comfort Inn. But it was there that Jacob met God — in a dream.

It's what happened next that is so unusual. Jacob saw a ladder between heaven and earth, with angels going back and forth. And God spoke to Jacob.

> I am the Lord, the God of Abraham your father and the God of Isaac; the land on which you lie I will give to you and to your offspring; and your offspring shall be like the dust of the earth, and you shall spread abroad to the west and to the east and to the north and to the south; and all the families

of the earth shall be blessed in you and in your offspring. Know that I am with you and will keep you wherever you go, and will bring you back to this land; for I will not leave you until I have done what I have promised you.

Wait a minute! I don't get it. God didn't slap Jacob's hands and tell him to shape up or he would burn in hell forever? This dirty little thief gets a blessing from God and a promise of land and descendants? That's what blows my mind. Jacob gets something totally undeserved and unearned. That's what we call 'grace.'

It's interesting to me that God didn't come to Jacob when he was awake, when Jacob was in control. God came to Jacob in a dream when Jacob was asleep. In other words, God was the one in control. Jacob did nothing to earn or deserve God's favor. Indeed, Jacob's behavior makes it ever so obvious that what God gave him came as pure gift, pure grace.

Do you see how this is so different from the ladder we talked about earlier? The ladder in Jacob's dream was not to help Jacob climb up to God. That ladder was for God to come down to Jacob. God came to Jacob and turned his world completely upside down with a gift of grace. God repeated to Jacob the promise made to his grandfather Abraham and to his father Isaac. But God also said something new to Jacob. God promised that he would be with Jacob, and that he would protect Jacob.

Jesus Christ is our ladder. In Jesus, God comes to us. We don't deserve anything from God. Like Jacob, we are sinners who often make a mess of our lives. But in grace, God comes to us. God claims us for himself. God gives us precious promises, words that can turn our world around and change our life forever. We need to hear those words over and over and let them sink deep into our hearts and minds.

Do you remember that song we sang — We are climbing Jacob's ladder? Every rung goes higher, higher, soldiers of the cross. The words really imply a sense of progress, don't they? We keep getting better and better, closer and closer to God. But that's not what the story is about. It's not about us and our efforts; it's all about God and God's grace. Martin Luther started out trying to climb that ladder. He tried harder than anyone to climb it. And then he learned the truth about God's gift in Jesus, and it changed his life. When Luther died, they discovered a piece of paper in his pocket with these words on them — "We are beggars. It is true." After a lifetime of serving God, Luther knew the truth. We don't get better and better. If anything, we become more and more dependent on God's grace. Beggars, it is true.

Jacob awoke from his dream a changed man. It was such a significant turning point in his life that he named that place Bethel — which means "the house of God." For us today, this is the house of God. God is here! Jesus is the ladder bringing God to us. God is present in the word proclaimed and in the bread and wine of Holy Communion. God is here today! Thanks be to God.

3. The Song — "All Are Welcome"

Proper 12 / Ordinary Time 17 — Genesis 29:15-28
"When The Trickster Got Tricked"

1. The Story

Reader: Then Laban said to Jacob,

Pastor: "Because you are my kinsman, should you therefore serve me for nothing? Tell me, what shall your wages be?"

Reader: Now Laban had two daughters; the name of the elder was Leah, and the name of the younger was Rachel. Leah's eyes were lovely, and Rachel was graceful and beautiful. Jacob loved Rachel; so he said,

All: "I will serve you seven years for your younger daughter Rachel."

Pastor: "It is better that I give her to you than that I should give her to any other man; stay with me."

Reader: So Jacob served seven years for Rachel, and they seemed to him but a few days because of the love he had for her. Then Jacob said to Laban,

All: "Give me my wife that I may go in to her, for my time is completed."

Reader: So Laban gathered together all the people of the place, and made a feast. But in the evening he took his daughter Leah and brought her to Jacob; and he went in to her. (Laban gave his maid Zilpah to his daughter Leah to be her maid.) When morning came, it was Leah! And Jacob said to Laban,

All: "What is this you have done to me? Did I not serve with you for Rachel? Why then have you deceived me?"

Pastor: "This is not done in our country — giving the younger before the firstborn. Complete the week of this one, and we will give you the other also in return for serving me another seven years."

Reader: Jacob did so, and completed her week; then Laban gave him his daughter Rachel as a wife." Word of God, word of life.

All: Thanks be to God.

2. The Sermon

Did any of you watch the O.J. Simpson parole hearings? I caught just a few minutes of them. What interested me was not so much O. J.'s answers, but the questions they asked him. I began to wonder, what is it like to be on a parole board? How do you assess if someone is ready for parole? What sort of things do you look for when evaluating someone? Obviously, you want to know if this person will be a threat to society. According to all the records, O.J. had been a model prisoner, cooperating with authorities and helping other prisoners. To me it seemed that what the parole board was looking for was the kind of impact nine years of incarceration had on O.J. Did he have remorse for his crime? Was he humbled or was he angry? Was he ready to be a responsible member of society? How had O.J. changed in prison?

I suppose most people have made up their minds whether they think O.J. was guilty or not for the 1994 murder of his wife, Nicole Brown Simpson. I'm guessing that when O.J. was found guilty of armed robbery in 2007, many people felt he had it coming for getting off with the murder of his wife. They felt that this time he was getting what he deserved, reaping what he had sowed. That was certainly my feeling. But as I watched O.J. respond to the questions of the parole board, I found myself starting to like the guy and have a little compassion for him. It was time to start a new chapter in the story of O.J. Simpson.

Our society has been caught up in this O.J. story ever since he won the Heisman trophy back in 1968. Since then he has gone from good to bad and everything in between. O.J. is a complicated character. One of the major parts in any good story is character development. Is a character believable? Is a character likable? Can you identify with him or her? Those are parts that make an interesting story.

Now keep this in mind as we look at the story of Jacob. When we look at the whole story from beginning to end, we see that there is some character development in Jacob. Jacob is born grabbing the heel of his brother. The name Jacob means heel-grabber or trickster. And he lived up to his name as an adult. But in our story today, we see the start of a change. The trickster gets tricked himself. Jacob gets a dose of his own medicine, and he doesn't like it. Next week we will hear the story of Jacob wrestling with God and being changed forever. In fact, the change is so significant that God gives him a new name: **Israel.**

I love these stories from Genesis, but there's a lot about them I don't understand. Our story today is about Jacob marrying two sisters, Leah and Rachel. I don't understand the marrying of many wives. I don't understand how women seem to be treated as property to be bartered for. I don't understand how a man can wake up the next morning after his wedding and realize he married the wrong woman. I may not like these parts of the story, but there are still parts of this story that we can learn from.

Earlier in Genesis we learned that Jacob had cheated his brother Esau, and then ran for his life to escape his brother's anger. I wonder if Jacob didn't have a change of heart on that long journey. Maybe he came to realize the error of his ways? I want to think that he wanted to change his life when he arrived at his uncle's home in a new land. Jacob fell in love with his cousin, Rachel, and agreed to work for his uncle for seven years for her. He worked hard and kept his word. I think he was really trying hard to change his ways. One of the most romantic verses in the whole Bible describes those seven years of waiting. "So Jacob served seven years for Rachel, and they seemed to him but a few days because of the love he had for her." Finally, the day arrived. There was a huge party late into the night. And Jacob took his wife to his tent. And they lived happily ever after. Not!

Jacob woke up to find he had been tricked. He had married the wrong woman. He was angry and went to his father-in-law. **"What is this you have done to me? Did I not serve with you for Rachel? Why then have you deceived me?"** Laban answered that it wasn't proper to marry the younger before the older. Work another seven years and Jacob could have the younger one too.

There is a certain justice in the story. The deceiver, Jacob, got deceived. The liar and cheater met his match. Did you notice how Jacob's punishment fit his earlier crime? They were both over issues of the first-born. Jacob tricked his first-born brother, Esau, and now he was tricked with his wife, the first-born sister, Leah.

I don't know how someone marries the wrong person. Obviously, there are ancient customs involved we aren't familiar with. It reminds me of a couple stories. I was touring Israel with a group. My daughter Siri was also on the tour. There was a time we were in Bethlehem and got off the bus. We were met by several locals trying to sell us stuff. One young man came up to me and pointed to Siri. "Is she your daughter?" he asked. I said yes and then the man said to me. "She is the most beautiful woman I have ever seen. I will give you 200 camels for her." I looked at him and said (tongue in cheek), "I won't take less than 500 camels for my daughter." My daughter was not amused. Women aren't property!

This Jacob story also reminds me of a hilarious commercial produced by a Norwegian bank a few years ago. A young woman wakes up in a strange bed and wonders where she is. She doesn't know how she got there. She looks around the room and doesn't recognize anything. It looks there has been a wild party. She stares in horror as she sees a huge wedding ring on her hand. There are pictures strewn about from the wedding. She finds a wedding dress and holds it up to her shoulders. How could this be? She remembers nothing. Just then a very handsome and sexy George Clooney walks in the room in his pajamas and says, "Hey there. I was letting you sleep." He walks over to kiss her and then takes her to his laptop and shows her a beautiful house that he was thinking about buying for them to live in. The woman can't believe what is happening to her. Then the screen goes blank and you see the words, "Some people have all the luck. For the rest of us, it would be wise to start saving." In other words, don't pin your hopes on marrying into a lot of money. Life doesn't work that way for most of us.

What's the point of our Jacob story? In some ways, we see Jacob's growth as a human being and as a person of faith. Jacob's scheming got him in trouble. It's true that in life we often reap what we sow. But there is the fact that God loved Jacob. Jacob didn't deserve it. God was with him in spite of his sins. God didn't abandon him. We see character development in Jacob. Jacob the trickster went from living for himself to living for something greater. We see Jacob grow and change.

Just like Jacob, we are all on a journey. We all are born with our own needs at the center of our lives. Some people call that, original sin. Somehow in our lives, we must learn empathy and compassion. We must learn to love. Our faith tells us that life works better when God and God's will for us is at the center of our lives. And God's will tells us to love our neighbors. For some of us, it takes a long time to learn that. Some never do learn that. But what helps us to learn that is when God's grace and God's love comes into our hearts undeserved. It has the power to humble us and change us. That's what God did for Jacob Israel. And that is what God has done for us in Jesus Christ.

Was O.J. guilty? At this point, the question is almost irrelevant. The bigger question is: what kind of person is O.J. now? I'm told that he led Bible studies in prison. I guess we will learn what kind of person he is over the next few years of his life. The important thing today, is that God's grace is for people like O.J., and God's grace is for you and me.

3. The Song — "God, When Human Bonds Are Broken"

Proper 13 / Ordinary Time 18 — Genesis 32:3-7a, 9-13, 22-31
"What's In A Name?"

1. The Story

Reader: Jacob sent messengers before him to his brother Esau in the land of Seir, the country of Edom, instructing them,

All: "Thus you shall say to my lord Esau: Thus says your servant Jacob, 'I have lived with Laban as an alien, and stayed until now; and I have oxen, donkeys, flocks, male and female slaves; and I have sent to tell my lord, in order that I may find favor in your sight.'"

Reader: The messengers returned to Jacob, saying, "We came to your brother Esau, and he is coming to meet you, and four hundred men are with him." Then Jacob was greatly afraid and distressed... And Jacob said,

All: "O God of my father Abraham and God of my father Isaac, O Lord who said to me, 'Return to your country and to your kindred, and I will do you good,' I am not worthy of the least of all the steadfast love and all the faithfulness that you have shown to your servant, for with only my staff I crossed this Jordan; and now I have become two companies. Deliver me, please, from the hand of my brother, from the hand of Esau, for I am afraid of him; he may come and kill us all, the mothers with the children. Yet you have said, 'I will surely do you good, and make your offspring as the sand of the sea, which cannot be counted because of their number.'"

Reader: So he spent that night there, and from what he had with him he took a present for his brother Esau, The same night he got up and took his two wives, his two maids, and his eleven children, and crossed the ford of the Jabbok. He took them and sent them across the stream, and likewise everything that he had. Jacob was left alone; and a man wrestled with him until daybreak. When the man saw that he did not prevail against Jacob, he struck him on the hip socket; and Jacob's hip was put out of joint as he wrestled with him. Then [the man] said,

Pastor: "Let me go, for the day is breaking."

All: "I will not let you go, unless you bless me."

Pastor: "What is your name?"

All: "Jacob."

Pastor: "You shall no longer be called Jacob, but Israel, for you have striven with God and with humans, and have prevailed."

All: "Please tell me your name."

Pastor: "Why is it that you ask my name?"

Reader: And there [the man] blessed him. So Jacob called the place Peniel, saying,

All: "For I have seen God face to face, and yet my life is preserved."

Reader: Word of God, word of life.

All: Thanks be to God.

2. The Sermon

If you've watched any news this week then you have seen a lot of the pope. Pope Francis has visited the US and it seems that there is pope fever. Francis is a rock star, the most popular pope in modern times. He has brought much change and excitement to the Roman Catholic Church, and indeed to people of faith everywhere. I have developed a deep respect for this humble servant of God.

I remember when Francis was elected Pope just over two years ago and we all were introduced to Cardinal Jorge Borgoglio. One of the papal traditions is that upon election the pope must choose a new name. Cardinal Borgoglio chose the name Francis, after St. Francis of Assisi. He was the first pope to choose that name, and it revealed a lot about the kind of Pope he intended to be. When you think of St. Francis, what do you think of? I think of someone who lived simply, who cared for the poor, and someone who loved nature. The opening hymn we sang, the words were written by St. Francis. Those are themes that we have heard Pope Francis emphasize over the last two years. Francis constantly reminds the world of the need to care for the poor, and to live simply. He demonstrates it by visiting the homeless, refusing to live in the papal mansion but instead a humble apartment. He carries his own suitcase. And when the pope arrived at the White House, it wasn't in a big expensive limousine, but a small Fiat. When he addressed Congress, Francis called on us to care for the earth in ways that improve it for future generations. Do you see how his ministry is embodied in the name he chose for himself — Francis?

A few weeks ago our story was about Jacob's father Isaac. The name **Isaac** means "laughter", and the story tells us how the laughter of skepticism became the laughter of joy. Today's story is contained in the name, **Jacob**. Jacob was a twin, born right after his brother Esau. In fact, the Bible says he was born grabbing on to his brother's heal. That's what the name Jacob literally means "heal grabber." It's almost as if the two brothers were fighting in the womb to see who would come out first. Esau won, but Jacob was right behind, as if he was refusing to submit to his older brother. Another way to translate the name Jacob is, "usurper." A usurper is someone who wrongfully takes someone else's place. And that is the meaning in this story. Jacob wanted the rights and privileges of the first-born. He was always plotting in the background, tricking his brother and deceiving his father. Jacob truly lived up to his name, and it got him into deep trouble.

Can you imagine growing up with a name like that? Jacob is a common and popular name today. But what if your name were liar, cheater, deceiver, or usurper? Wouldn't it impact how you look at life and how you thought and felt about yourself? We are given names by our parents. Most of us don't even know what they mean. But many of us are given nicknames by our friends or colleagues. Sometimes the names we are given express affection and love. I think of one of my mentors from college days. We all lovingly called him "Doc." To this day I can't imagine calling him by his first name. He will always be "Doc" to me because he has a special place in my heart. I'm sure many of you have nicknames that people have used to show you affection and acceptance.

Several years ago there was a survey done of children asking them to define love. One four-year-old boy had something rather profound to say. "When someone loves you, the way they say your name is different. You know that your name is safe in their mouth."[12] It's obvious that this little boy had experienced that in his life. He knew when people used his name in ways that communicated love. He also knew when people used his name to demean and belittle.

Sometimes the names we are given in life aren't very nice. Those names are meant to demean, belittle and putdown. I wonder if some of you don't bear wounds and scars from the names you've been given over the years. Sometimes we allow those names to have way too much power in our lives, to define us to the point that we forget our real names and our real identities.

Back to our Jacob story! Jacob the heal grabber had to flee for his life. His brother Esau was angry enough to kill him. Jacob lived in exile for fourteen years. When he finally returned home, I'm sure he was hoping that his brother had forgiven him. That's where we pick up the story today. The night before he was to meet his brother, Jacob was plagued by fears and doubts. Jacob the deceiver, the usurper, was reaping all that he had sown. Have you ever been unable to sleep, tossing and turning in your bed, troubled by your worries and fears or by guilt? That's what Jacob was doing. It says that he wrestled all night long with a man. Jacob, who wrestled with his brother Esau in his mother's womb,

12 Author unknown.

did what he did best, wrestling and conniving his way through life. Only this time Jacob wrestled with God, and it would change him forever. In an act of grace, God blessed Jacob and gave him a new name, "Israel." No longer was he to be called Jacob the heel-grabber, the deceiver and usurper. From now on, he was Israel, one who wrestles with God.

The South Dakota State Penitentiary has a congregation that meets for weekly worship. Whenever I go to worship with the inmates, there is something that stands out to me loud and clear. The uniforms the prisoners wear are bright orange with big letters on the back and leg that say, "INMATE." According to society and the state, that is who they are — inmate. There in prison their identity and names are stripped away, and they are given a new name and identity — inmate. But for that hour in worship, they get to hear the good news and be reminded that inmate is not their true name and it isn't their true identity. There in worship they are reminded that they are children of God, beloved by God.

We come here each week to worship to be reminded of the same thing. Just as Jacob was given a new name and identity we too are given a new name in the waters of baptism — child of God. We aren't just who our parents have called us. And we aren't who the world calls us. When the world tries to press us into its mold and define us, that's when we need to be reminded who we really are, who God says we are. We are first and foremost who God calls us — sinners saved by God's grace in Jesus Christ, children of God. It's so easy to forget that and start to believe the lies others want to say about us. But I'd rather listen to God than anyone else.

Our calling is to leave this place having been reminded who we are and having been blessed by God, and then to bring God's blessing to others. Pope Francis chose that name because he wanted to bring a blessing to the poor. God gives us our names, child of God, so that we can bring God's blessing to others. Throughout this week, I hope you will find ways to speak a blessing to others. Call them by name and remind them of the name God has given them — child of God.

I'm going to end this sermon a little differently than usual. I'm going to ask you to practice blessing one another. I want you to find another person and say these words to each other, taking turns. #1 — I will not let you go, until you bless me. #2 — You are a beloved child of God.

3. The Song — "If You But Trust In God To Guide You"

Proper 14 / Ordinary Time 19 — Genesis 37:1-14, 18-28
"When Bad Things Happen"

1. The Story

Reader: Jacob settled in the land where his father had lived as an alien, the land of Canaan. This is the story of the family of Jacob. Joseph, being seventeen years old, was shepherding the flock with his brothers; he was a helper to the sons of Bilhah and Zilpah, his father's wives; and Joseph brought a bad report of them to their father. Now Israel loved Joseph more than any other of his children, because he was the son of his old age; and he had made him a long robe with sleeves. But when his brothers saw that their father loved him more than all his brothers, they hated him, and could not speak peaceably to him. Once Joseph had a dream, and when he told it to his brothers, they hated him even more. He said to them,

All: "Listen to this dream that I dreamed. There we were, binding sheaves in the field. Suddenly my sheaf rose and stood upright; then your sheaves gathered around it, and bowed down to my sheaf."

Reader: His brothers said to him,

Pastor: "Are you indeed to reign over us? Are you indeed to have dominion over us?"

Reader: So they hated him even more because of his dreams and his words. He had another dream, and told it to his brothers, saying,

All: "Look, I have had another dream: the sun, the moon, and eleven stars were bowing down to me."

Reader: But when he told it to his father and to his brothers, his father rebuked him, and said to him,

Pastor: "What kind of dream is this that you have had? Shall we indeed come, I and your mother and your brothers, and bow to the ground before you?"

Reader: So his brothers were jealous of him, but his father kept the matter in mind. Now his brothers went to pasture their father's flock near Shechem. And Israel said to Joseph,

Pastor: "Are not your brothers pasturing the flock at Shechem? Come, I will send you to them."

All: "Here I am."

Pastor: "Go now, see if it is well with your brothers and with the flock; and bring word back to me."

Reader: So he sent him from the valley of Hebron. He came to Shechem.... They saw him from a distance, and before he came near to them, they conspired to kill him. They said to one another,

Pastor: "Here comes this dreamer. Come now, let us kill him and throw him into one of the pits; then we shall say that a wild animal has devoured him, and we shall see what will become of his dreams."

Reader: But when Reuben heard it, he delivered him out of their hands, saying,

Pastor: "Let us not take his life... Shed no blood; throw him into this pit here in the wilderness, but lay no hand on him"

Reader: [He said that] — that he might rescue him out of their hand and restore him to his father. So when Joseph came to his brothers, they stripped him of his robe, the long robe with sleeves that he wore; and they took him and threw him into a pit. The pit was empty; there was no water in it. Then they sat down to eat; and looking up they saw a caravan of Ishmaelites coming from Gilead, with their camels carrying gum, balm, and resin, on their way to carry it down to Egypt. Then Judah said to his brothers,

Pastor: "What profit is it if we kill our brother and conceal his blood? Come, let us sell him to the Ishmaelites, and not lay our hands on him, for he is our brother, our own flesh."

Reader: And his brothers agreed. When some Midianite traders passed by, they drew Joseph up, lifting him out of the pit, and sold him to the Ishmaelites for twenty pieces of silver. And they took Joseph to Egypt." Word of God, word of life.

All: Thanks be to God.

2. The Sermon

Several years ago a book came out that quickly became a best seller. It was titled *When Bad Things Happen to Good People* written by Rabbi Harold Kushner. In the book he struggled to make sense out of the death of his son who died of a terrible disease. We all struggle to make sense of suffering when it comes. We ask the question — Why? Why is this happening to me? Does God even care about my pain?

I think it's precisely this question that the story of Joseph was designed to answer. Of all the stories in the Bible this story is my favorite. A few years ago, I took my kids to see the musical based on this story — *Joseph and the Amazing Technicolor Dreamcoat*. It's a great musical with many fun songs. But it amazed me as I listened to the musical that not once did the author mention God. In our politically correct environment he made it into a rags-to-riches story, a tale of overcoming adversity and fulfilling your dreams. It's obvious because of the musical's popularity that it's a story that speaks to many people today. But I want to invite you into the real Joseph story, a story that is so much more profound and meaningful for our lives today.

I want to explore this story in four scenes. Scene One, let's call Sibling Rivalry. Joseph grew up in a large family — there were twelve sons. I can't imagine a family with twelve boys without some fighting going on. What made it worse was that Joseph was the favorite son and got special treatment from his dad. Because of that, Joseph grew arrogant. He had feelings of superiority toward his brothers. As you read the story you can feel the tension in the family. Verse four says, **"But when his brothers saw that their father loved him more than all his brothers, they hated him, and could not speak peaceably to him."** So what happens in a family environment like that? The story continues. One day Joseph came to visit his brothers when they were tending the herds in the field, far away from Mom and Dad's protection. They ripped his coat off him and threw him in a pit to die. Then they put some blood on his coat, this special coat their father had given Joseph, and brought it back to Jacob saying they had found it and that Joseph must have been killed by a wild animal. Jacob almost died from his grief and shock. Though his brothers were glad to be rid of Joseph, some of them felt enough guilt to return to the pit and sell Joseph off to some traders who were traveling to Egypt.

Does that sound like some families you have known? We all know families that fight with each other, siblings who fight when they think they're not getting their fair share. Maybe it's fighting over the division of an inheritance. I know of two brothers who had a fight and refused to speak to each other the rest of their lives. Maybe I'm describing your family right now. Every family has its times of tension when members don't get along with each other. What we need to know is that God cares about families like this. This story tells us that God is not absent from our conflicts but cares deeply about us and our well-being.

In Scene Two the action switches from the land of Israel to Egypt. Being sold into slavery and exiled from his home was not a good thing for Joseph. The Bible is very clear in saying that in spite of the evil Joseph experienced God was with him. He was purchased as a slave by Potiphar, an officer of Pharaoh, the captain of the guard. Potiphar took a liking to Joseph because he saw him to be intelligent and hardworking. Read with me Genesis 39:1-4.

"Now Joseph was taken down to Egypt, and Potiphar, an officer of Pharaoh, the captain of the guard, an Egyptian, bought him from the Ishmaelites who had brought him down there. The LORD was with Joseph, and he became a successful man; he was in the house of his Egyptian master. His master saw that the LORD was with him, and that the LORD caused all that he did to prosper in his hands. So Joseph found favor in his sight and attended him; he made him overseer of his house and put him in charge of all that he had."

In spite of all that had happened to him Joseph didn't lose his faith in God. And God blessed Joseph's faith and obedience by prospering him. Scene Two we could call The Rewards of Integrity.

Potiphar was a busy and important man; he didn't have a lot of time for his wife. And since Joseph spent so much time in the home and was handsome, it wasn't long before lonely Potiphar's wife began to desire him and one day commanded him to lie with her. But Joseph refused. Read with me his response in verses 8-9.

But he refused and said to his master's wife, "Look, with me here, my master has no concern about anything in the house, and he has put everything that he has in my hand. He is not greater in this house than I am, nor has he kept back anything from me except yourself, because you are his wife. How then could I do this great wickedness, and sin against God?

Did you notice what Joseph didn't say? He didn't say it would be a sin against *Potiphar* to lie with his wife, but it was a sin against **God**. We live in a sex saturated culture today where sexual fulfillment is seen as entitlement for everyone. The creed of our culture today is "if it feels good, do it." As long as it's two consenting adults and no one is hurt whatever you want to do is okay and it's no one's business but your own. But that wasn't Joseph's attitude. He called a spade a spade. It was a sin against God. Joseph was a man of faith and integrity and so he refused this invitation. Day after day this temptation went on until one day Potiphar's wife got tired of being rejected and she grabbed his robe and tore it off him. When Joseph ran away naked she screamed rape. No questions were asked — Joseph was arrested and thrown in prison.

Let's call Scene Three When Bad Things Happen To Good People. Joseph's faith must have been sorely tested. Here he had followed the rules, lived with purity and integrity, and yet ended up in prison. Everything he had worked hard for was gone. Where was God now? What was the use in being good and in obeying God? I can just imagine that Joseph must have struggled with questions like that. Kind of like the questions you and I struggle with when life isn't fair. But even as he languished in prison the Bible says that God was with Joseph. Read with me 39:20-23.

And Joseph's master took him and put him into the prison, the place where the king's prisoners were confined; he remained there in prison. But the LORD was with Joseph and showed him steadfast love; he gave him favor in the sight of the chief jailer. The chief jailer committed to Joseph's care all the prisoners who were in the prison, and whatever was done there, he was the one who did it. The chief jailer paid no heed to anything that was in Joseph's care, because the LORD was with him; and whatever he did, the LORD made it prosper.

God didn't give up on Joseph, and Joseph didn't give up on God. He clung to his faith even in the most trying circumstances.

In prison, Joseph gained a reputation as someone who could interpret dreams. One day Pharaoh had some dreams that troubled him, and he called for all the wise men to come and interpret the dreams for him. But none of them could interpret the dreams to his satisfaction. It was then that someone told Pharaoh about Joseph. Joseph was led out of prison and into Pharaoh's presence. Pharaoh told him the dreams and Joseph interpreted them. Egypt would have seven years of plenty followed by seven

79

years of famine. Not only did Joseph tell Pharaoh what was going to happen, but he also suggested a plan of action. Pharaoh was so impressed with Joseph that he promoted him to the position of governor in charge of the new food storage program. Joseph went from rags to riches in one day.

Scene Four we'll call: God's Purpose Is Worked Out. When the famine hit Egypt it also hit Israel. Jacob and his family grew hungry and after hearing there was food in Egypt he sent his sons down there to buy some. Little did they know they would encounter their brother Joseph there. The story takes several twists and turns but eventually Joseph revealed himself to his brothers. Let's read together Joseph's moving speech in 45:4-8.

> Then Joseph said to his brothers, "Come closer to me." And they came closer. He said, "I am your brother, Joseph, whom you sold into Egypt. And now do not be distressed, or angry with yourselves, because you sold me here; for God sent me before you to preserve life. For the famine has been in the land these two years; and there are five more years in which there will be neither plowing nor harvest. God sent me before you to preserve for you a remnant on earth, and to keep alive for you many survivors. So it was not you who sent me here, but God; he has made me a father to Pharaoh and lord of all his house and ruler over all the land of Egypt.

It's obvious that Joseph reflected back on his life and sensed God's presence and hand leading and preparing him for just such a time. Years later, after his father Jacob died, his brothers wondered whether Joseph had really forgiven them. Joseph reassured them that though they had meant only evil to him, God had turned it around to bring a greater good.

There's so much more to this ancient story. It's a great story that tells us about the kind of God we follow today. It's a story that comforts us when we suffer or feel that nothing is going right in our lives. It's a story that gives us hope by showing us that God is wise and powerful and can bring good out of bad. That's the real message in this story. God's power is seen working behind the scenes taking evil and bringing some good effect. I don't mean to suggest a simplistic idea like there's a silver lining in every cloud. I also don't mean to suggest that God is controlling everything that happens to us, both the good and the bad things that cause us pain. Sin is sin and its impact in our lives hurts us and others powerfully. We don't blame God for that. We don't blame God for cancer when it strikes. We don't blame God for the drunk driver that kills someone. We don't blame God for terrorists that fly planes into buildings. But the message here is that somehow God is able to take that evil, transform it, and bring something good out of it. That is precisely the power and the sovereignty of God, that God can take what we intend for evil and turn it on its head so that something good results. That's what God did with Joseph. That's what God can do in your life and mine. Romans 8:28 says, **"We know that all things work together for good for those who love God, who are called according to his purpose."** Isn't that what God did in Jesus. God didn't nail Jesus on the cross. It was an evil act done by human beings. And yet through that act, God was able to accomplish a great work — the salvation of the world. Through Jesus' death and resurrection our sin is forgiven and our relationship with God restored.

Looking back over his life Joseph saw how God was with him. Maybe you can't see it now, but some day you'll look back over the events of your life and see that God really was there in times of greatest need and pain, and out of that pain God was able to bring something good. Have patience. Trust in God's love for you.

3. The Song — "How Firm A Foundation"

Proper 15 / Ordinary Time 20 — Genesis 45:1-15
"The Power Of Forgiveness"

1. The Story

Reader: Then Joseph could no longer control himself before all those who stood by him, and he cried out,

Pastor: "Send everyone away from me."

Reader: So no one stayed with him when Joseph made himself known to his brothers. And he wept so loudly that the Egyptians heard it, and the household of Pharaoh heard it. Joseph said to his brothers,

Pastor: "I am Joseph. Is my father still alive?"

Reader: But his brothers could not answer him, so dismayed were they at his presence. Then Joseph said to his brothers,

Pastor: "Come closer to me."

Reader: And they came closer. He said,

Pastor: "I am your brother, Joseph, whom you sold into Egypt. And now do not be distressed, or angry with yourselves, because you sold me here; for God sent me before you to preserve life. For the famine has been in the land these two years; and there are five more years in which there will be neither plowing nor harvest. God sent me before you to preserve for you a remnant on earth, and to keep alive for you many survivors. So it was not you who sent me here, but God; he has made me a father to Pharaoh and lord of all his house and ruler over all the land of Egypt. Hurry and go up to my father and say to him, 'Thus says your son Joseph, God has made me lord of all Egypt; come down to me, do not delay. You shall settle in the land of Goshen, and you shall be near me, you and your children and your children's children, as well as your flocks, your herds, and all that you have. I will provide for you there — since there are five more years of famine to come — so that you and your household, and all that you have, will not come to poverty.' And now your eyes and the eyes of my brother Benjamin see that it is my own mouth that speaks to you. You must tell my father how greatly I am honored in Egypt, and all that you have seen. Hurry and bring my father down here."

Reader: Then he fell upon his brother Benjamin's neck and wept, while Benjamin wept upon his neck. And he kissed all his brothers and wept upon them; and after that his brothers talked with him." Word of God, word of life.

All: Thanks be to God.

2. The Sermon

Life often takes unexpected turns and twists, doesn't it? How many of you at the beginning of your life would have scripted your life the way it turned out? We start our lives with so many hopes and dreams. For some of us, life turns out the way we plan and envision it. But I think that for most of us, life turns out very differently than we wanted. Let's imagine for a moment that there is a book with your name written on it — The Story Of Rolf Svanoe. It's your story and you get to write it. Chapter one, Rolf is born. Chapter two, Rolf grows up in a loving home. Chapter three, Rolf goes off to college and chooses a career. Chapter four, Rolf marries the love of his life. Chapter five, Rolf has a family and watches his kids grow up in a loving home. Chapter six, Rolf is blessed with several grandchildren. Chapter seven, Rolf retires after a long and successful career. Chapter eight, Rolf enjoys good health into his nineties. Chapter nine, Rolf dies after a long and happy life, but not before the Minnesota Vikings win the Superbowl. Isn't that the way most of us would choose to script our lives? Rarely does it turn out the way we want. The story can get changed by any number of things.

- An unplanned pregnancy.
- An accident that leaves you permanently disabled.
- A diagnosis of cancer or other disease.
- Depression or mental illness.
- A stock market crash that takes most of your savings.
- War.
- An unhappy marriage that ends in divorce.
- Loss of a job.
- Being the victim of crime or discrimination.

You could add any number of things to this list. I guess the lesson is that as hard as we try to plan our lives, there are times we don't get to write the story. Life writes the story for us. We can't control many of the things that happen to us. The one thing we can control is how we react when life goes bad. Will we respond with anger and bitterness? Or will we respond with love and forgiveness? Will we choose to see the glass as half-empty or half-full? And where does God fit into all of this?

The book of Genesis contains the story of Joseph. More time and attention is given to his life than any other person in Genesis. Joseph had big dreams for his life. Even though he was the youngest of twelve boys, he dreamt that he would rule over his brothers someday. His brothers hated him for it. It's the same story we saw earlier in Jacob and Esau, the younger wanting to rule over the older. It's not too surprising that Joseph would take after his dear old Dad. Joseph wasn't very likeable as a teenager. He was a snitch, a tattle-tale. He was his father's favorite and tried to use that to his advantage with his brothers. His actions made enemies of his brothers. So one day they decided to get rid of him. They sold him into slavery and told his father that an animal had killed him. Joseph ended up in Egypt, where he ended up in a position of power. He was put in charge of the Egypt's equivalent of FEMA — Famine Emergency Management Agency, and stockpiled food to face the upcoming shortage. Later, when Joseph's brothers came to Egypt seeking to buy food, Joseph realized that God was somehow using Joseph's position to provide for his family and to insure their survival. Somehow, looking back over his life, Joseph could see the hand of God. Joseph could have been very angry at the way his life turned out — being sold into slavery and then doing prison time after being falsely accused of a crime. But the story tells us several times that the Lord was with Joseph (39:2, 21). Joseph chose to forgive his brothers and provide for them.

The story of Joseph leads us to ask questions about God and how God is involved in the world. There are some who would say that God was in control of everything, guiding all the events in order to accomplish God's purpose. God was in control of every aspect of Joseph's life, leading everything to the end result that God's chosen people did not starve to death. Many people find comfort in this. "God is in control," we often hear people say. Especially when life doesn't make any sense, if we believe that God understands and has a plan, that is something that helps us to cope. There is comfort in believing in a loving heavenly Father who is controlling everything quietly in the background, even if we can't understand it.

The problem with this is that we want to give God credit for the good, but not the blame for the bad. Do we really want to believe that God controls everything that happens when a child dies in an accident or a spouse dies of cancer? Do we really want to believe that God was in control when a terrorist ran a van into pedestrians in Barcelona? Do we really want to believe that God controls everything when six million Jews are murdered or that in 2021 human beings are still bought and sold as slaves? Is God in control of everything that happens in our world today?

Romans 8:28 is a verse that people often turn to for help in thinking about God's involvement with the world. **"We know that all things work together for good for those who love God, who are called according to his purpose."** It doesn't say that God is controlling everything that happens. It says that God is able to take the evil in this world and make something good out of it in the end. Even in a world that is opposed to God, even with people who rebel against God's will, in the midst of random accidents and terrible evil and violence, God is still able to accomplish God's purpose.

I wonder if the apostle Paul didn't have the Joseph story in mind when he wrote that verse? Joseph discovered it to be true. At least that is how the story ends. But I wonder how Joseph felt after being stripped and beaten by his brothers, and left for dead at the bottom of a pit? Do you suppose he looked up through the hole far above him to the sky and angrily prayed to God. "God, why did you do this to me?" And what does God say to Joseph? "Trust me, Joe. I've got a plan. Everything's under control." Or does God say to Joseph, "Life isn't fair, Joe. Don't blame me. Frankly, a lot of this mess is of your own doing. But I do love you. Let's see if we can make something good come out of all this, but I want you to trust me and keep the faith." Joseph did keep the faith. He was humbled by his experiences in life. And at the end of the story, when he met his brothers again, he chose to forgive the evil they had done to him.

Does the story of Joseph sound like any other story you know from the New Testament? Joseph is a type of Christ. Joseph was the victim of evil circumstances and yet God raised him up and exalted him to save his people from famine. Jesus was the victim of evil circumstances and yet God raised him from the dead in order to save his people from their sin. Do you see how the Joseph story foreshadows the story of salvation in Jesus?

There are times in life when we, like Joseph, are at the bottom of the pit looking up to God and asking, "Why?" We may never get a satisfactory answer, some over-arching plan or reason that makes sense to us of our suffering. While God may not give us an answer to our questions, God is with us in our suffering, just like God was with Joseph. God is with us in Jesus, hanging on the cross. God weeps with us, cares for us especially when we are at the bottom of the pit. We cling in hope to a God who is able to turn death into resurrection. God will not be undone by the events that may come our way in life. Somehow God can and will make all things work together for good in the end. God invites us to keep the faith, to choose love over hatred, to choose forgiveness over revenge. God invites us to have compassion for the victims, the hungry and the poor, and to speak out on their behalf. This is the way of Joseph and of Jesus.

Life's story can sometimes be filled with a lot of hell. With God's love and forgiveness, that same story can turn into a little bit of heaven.

3. The Song — "What God Ordains Is Good Indeed"

Proper 16 / Ordinary Time 21 — Exodus 1:8-2:10
"Disobeying Pharaoh's Command"

1. The Story

Reader: A new king arose over Egypt, who did not know Joseph. He said to his people,

Pastor: "Look, the Israelite people are more numerous and more powerful than we. Come, let us deal shrewdly with them, or they will increase and, in the event of war, join our enemies and fight against us and escape from the land."

Reader: Therefore they set taskmasters over them to oppress them with forced labor. They built supply cities, Pithom and Rameses, for Pharaoh. But the more they were oppressed, the more they multiplied and spread, so that the Egyptians came to dread the Israelites. The Egyptians became ruthless in imposing tasks on the Israelites, and made their lives bitter with hard service in mortar and brick and in every kind of field labor. They were ruthless in all the tasks that they imposed on them. The king of Egypt said to the Hebrew midwives, one of whom was named Shiphrah and the other Puah,

Pastor: "When you act as midwives to the Hebrew women, and see them on the birthstool, if it is a boy, kill him; but if it is a girl, she shall live."

Reader: But the midwives feared God; they did not do as the king of Egypt commanded them, but they let the boys live. So the king of Egypt summoned the midwives and said to them,

Pastor: "Why have you done this, and allowed the boys to live?"

Reader: The midwives said to Pharaoh,

All: "Because the Hebrew women are not like the Egyptian women; for they are vigorous and give birth before the midwife comes to them."

Reader: So God dealt well with the midwives; and the people multiplied and became very strong. And because the midwives feared God, he gave them families. Then Pharaoh commanded all his people,

Pastor: "Every boy that is born to the Hebrews you shall throw into the Nile, but you shall let every girl live."

Reader: Now a man from the house of Levi went and married a Levite woman. The woman conceived and bore a son; and when she saw that he was a fine baby, she hid him three months. When she could hide him no longer she got a papyrus basket for him, and plastered it with bitumen and pitch; she put the child in it and placed it among the reeds on the bank of the river. His sister stood at a distance, to see what would happen to him. The daughter of Pharaoh came down to bathe at the river, while her attendants walked beside the river. She saw the basket among the reeds and sent her maid to bring it. When she opened it, she saw the child. He was crying, and she took pity on him,

Pastor: "This must be one of the Hebrews' children,"

Reader: Then his sister said to Pharaoh's daughter,

All: "Shall I go and get you a nurse from the Hebrew women to nurse the child for you?"

Reader: Pharaoh's daughter said to her,

Pastor: "Yes."

Reader: So the girl went and called the child's mother. Pharaoh's daughter said to her,

Pastor: "Take this child and nurse it for me, and I will give you your wages."

Reader: So the woman took the child and nursed it. When the child grew up, she brought him to Pharaoh's daughter, and she took him as her son. She named him Moses,

Pastor: "because, I drew him out of the water."

Reader: Word of God, word of life.

All: Thanks be to God.

2. The Sermon

It's always interesting to travel to another country and experience life that is different from what we experience here in the US. Norway is a wealthy country ever since oil was discovered in 1969. Since then Norway has been very frugal investing its money and also investing in the country's infrastructure. Norway has high taxes, but people get a lot from their government, like free health care and education, generous vacations and work environments. In fact, just this year Norway came in first place on the United Nations World Happiness Report.

Not everyone is happy in Norway, however. I met relatives who are angry at Norway's immigration policy. Specifically, they are angry that many immigrants are refusing to assimilate and learn Norwegian language and culture. There is growing anger and ill will especially toward Muslims and a real distrust that Norwegian generosity is being taken advantage of. Those feelings can easily degrade into racism.

These are tensions that we are feeling in our country as well. Who do we allow into our country? Do we require them to assimilate and learn English? We want to keep terrorists out, but what about homegrown terrorists? Who can we trust? How do we go about our lives without being racist? And how can we be a country that isn't determined by our fears, but by our hopes and our ideals? Those ideals are enshrined on the Statue of Liberty.

Give me your tired, your poor,
Your huddled masses yearning to breathe free,
The wretched refuse of your teeming shore.
Send these, the homeless, tempest-tossed to me,
I lift my lamp beside the golden door![13]

These aren't new issues facing us. They are as old as the Bible. Last Sunday we finished the book of Genesis with the story of Joseph and how God's people came to Egypt. They were immigrants who were welcomed into the country. But now this week we begin the book of Exodus a few hundred years later and the Hebrew people were in a different situation. They were an oppressed minority. A new king rose to power that didn't know the history and only saw the Hebrew people as a despised minority and threat to his future. He suspected that they were terrorists who had no loyalty to Pharaoh or Egypt. What was he to do? Pharaoh decided to let fear determine his politics. He controlled the Hebrews by enslaving them. Oppressed people who have heavy forced labor don't have time or energy to fight back. And besides, Pharaoh was getting some serious infrastructure building done. Cities were getting built with cheap labor. But Pharaoh's fears grew of the Hebrew people and he began to order a genocide. Kill all the male babies when they are born. That's one way to control the Hebrew minority. And that is where we encounter our story today.

We usually call this story "The Birth of Moses" and we focus on this little baby floating down the Nile River in a homemade basket. But Moses is not the major character in this story. He's just a baby. I suppose we could say he was a "basket case." Did you notice that all the heroes in this story are women? We have the Hebrew midwives who engaged in civil disobedience, refusing to follow Pharaoh's evil order. Do you know who Shiphrah and Puah are? It's interesting to me that their names are preserved by

13 Emma Lazarus, 'The New Colossus', Statue of Liberty National Monument, 10 <https://www.nps.gov/stli/learn/historyculture/colossus.htm> [15 August 2020]

the storyteller when so many women in the Bible are nameless. We don't name our daughters Shiphrah or Puah, and yet they are the heroines in this story. They chose to follow God instead of fear, instead of an evil, racist ideology.

There's a popular video making the rounds on the internet. It tells the World War Two story of Sir Nicholas Winton, a British citizen. Around Christmastime 1938, instead of going on a vacation to Switzerland like most of his wealthy banker friends did, Sir Winton decided to go to Prague and set up a refugee system for Jewish children at risk from the Nazis. He and his mother saved 669 children from the Nazi death camps. Some fifty years later, Sir Winton was invited to the taping of a BBC program called "That's Life." He was just sitting in the audience when the host of the show asked a simple question: "Is there anyone in the audience tonight who owes their life to Nicholas Winton?" All the children he had saved fifty years earlier were sitting in the audience **right next to him the whole time**. Half the people in the theater stood up. Sir Winton was overcome by emotion. It is a powerful story of the difference that one or two people can make, all because they refuse to follow unjust laws, and to let hatred and fear determine their lives.

I'm sure that many of you have been dismayed and horrified by the violence and racism on display in Charlottesville a few years ago. This does not represent the ideals and values of our country. It certainly does not represent the beliefs and values of our church. I want to read to you from a statement issued by our church in response:

> The Evangelical Lutheran Church in America (ELCA), stands against all forms of hatred and discrimination. The church believes that cultural, ethnic and racial differences should be seen and celebrated as what God intends them to be — blessings rather than means of oppression and discrimination. The ELCA's social statement [on racism] states: "Racism — a mix of power, privilege, and prejudice — is sin, a violation of God's intention for humanity. The resulting racial, ethnic or cultural barriers deny the truth that all people are God's creatures and, therefore, persons of dignity.

Racism fractures and fragments both church and society."[14]

Our presiding bishop, Elizabeth Eaton, also issued a statement saying, "We recognize that the kind of violence we witnessed in Charlottesville last weekend is very real and affects all of us. We need to stand up firmly against racism and anti-Semitism, show up for and advocate with others. Jesus, who makes visible those who are invisible, is already there. We need to show up, and we need to listen in each of our communities."

As Christians living today, we are called to be like Shiphrah and Puah. Indeed, we are called to be like Jesus and to reject violence and hatred and confront it with compassion and forgiveness. We are called to "love our enemies and pray for those who persecute" us. And when people around us are victims, we are called to stand by their side and add our voices to theirs.

God in Jesus Christ loves you, forgives you, sees in you something worth saving. And now he asks us to do the same for our neighbor, especially the neighbor who is different from us.

3. The Song — "O God Of Every Nation"

---

14 Evangelical Lutheran Church in America, "A Social Statement on: Freed In Christ: Race, Ethnicity, and Culture." Adopted by the third Churchwide Assembly on August 31, 1993. Accessed 15 August 2020. https://elca.org/Faith/Faith-and-Society/Social-Statements/Race-Ethnicity-and-Culture

Proper 17 / Ordinary Time 22 — Exodus 3:1-15
"When God Hears Our Cries"

1. The Story

Reader: Moses was keeping the flock of his father-in-law Jethro, the priest of Midian; he led his flock beyond the wilderness, and came to Horeb, the mountain of God. There the angel of the Lord appeared to him in a flame of fire out of a bush; he looked, and the bush was blazing, yet it was not consumed. Then Moses said,

All: "I must turn aside and look at this great sight, and see why the bush is not burned up."

Reader: When the Lord saw that he had turned aside to see, God called to him out of the bush,

Pastor: "Moses, Moses!"

All: "Here I am."

Pastor: "Come no closer! Remove the sandals from your feet, for the place on which you are standing is holy ground... I am the God of your father, the God of Abraham, the God of Isaac, and the God of Jacob."

Reader: And Moses hid his face, for he was afraid to look at God. Then the Lord said,

Pastor: "I have observed the misery of my people who are in Egypt; I have heard their cry on account of their taskmasters. Indeed, I know their sufferings, and I have come down to deliver them from the Egyptians, and to bring them up out of that land to a good and broad land, a land flowing with milk and honey, to the country of the Canaanites, the Hittites, the Amorites, the Perizzites, the Hivites, and the Jebusites. The cry of the Israelites has now come to me; I have also seen how the Egyptians oppress them. So come, I will send you to Pharaoh to bring my people, the Israelites, out of Egypt."

All: "Who am I that I should go to Pharaoh, and bring the Israelites out of Egypt?"

Pastor: "I will be with you; and this shall be the sign for you that it is I who sent you: when you have brought the people out of Egypt, you shall worship God on this mountain."

All: "If I come to the Israelites and say to them, 'The God of your ancestors has sent me to you,' and they ask me, 'What is his name?' what shall I say to them?"

Pastor: "I AM WHO I AM... Thus you shall say to the Israelites, 'I AM has sent me to you... The Lord, the God of your ancestors, the God of Abraham, the God of Isaac, and the God of Jacob, has sent me to you': This is my name forever, and this my title for all generations."

Reader: Word of God, word of life.

All: Thanks be to God.

2. The Sermon

It has been a momentous week. Who hasn't been shocked by the images in the news of the devastation from Hurricane Harvey? It is the largest natural disaster in US history. 41 people died; hundreds of thousands lost their homes. As people returned to their homes and saw the extent of the damage, there was growing despair. How would they recover?

While we've seen the worst in nature, we've also seen the best in the human spirit. The nation has come together to meet this crisis. Who hasn't been impressed by the first responders, the volunteers showing up with their boats to do water rescues, the helicopter rescues pulling people off their roofs to safety.

It reminds me of the movie, *Dunkirk*. Did any of you see it? It's an amazing true story from WWII. British private citizens responded to a call to cross the English Channel to rescue the British Army stranded on the shallow beach of Dunkirk. The British Royal Navy ships were too big, so a flotilla of pleasure boats made the crossing and moved the soldiers back to safety. They would all certainly have been killed by the Germans without that help.

There is something clarifying about human tragedy. It is like a call from God to respond to human need. There is no debate, no partisan politics, only human need crying out for help. And people responded. In this tragedy, there weren't Republicans or Democrats, Christians, Muslim, or atheist, Blacks, Whites, or Latinos, poor people or wealthy people. They were just human beings in need, and other human beings responding to that need out of compassion and empathy.

I remember watching some of those helicopter rescues and seeing the reactions of people to being saved from the flood waters, especially when they were reunited with family. There were spontaneous expressions of praise to God and singing. "Thank You, Jesus. God Is So Good." And I remember thinking, "Yes, God is good. But it was that helicopter crew who rescued you and your Momma." But the more I thought about it, the more I realized, they were right. It was God who rescued them. It was God moving in the hearts of ordinary people, calling them to respond to the cry for help. God is love, the Bible tells us. And when people are hurting, God will move in our hearts filling us with love and compassion to respond to the cries of our hurting neighbor.

This is the situation we find in our story from Exodus. God's people were brutally oppressed by the Egyptian empire. It wasn't just Pharaoh, but a whole racist ideology that allowed a people to be enslaved and sentenced to hard labor. And God's people cried out in pain.

And where was God? God was not distant and unaffected. Listen again to what God said to Moses, and pay attention to the verbs. **"Then the Lord said, 'I have *observed* the misery of my** people who are in Egypt; I have *heard* their cry on account of their taskmasters. Indeed, I *know* their sufferings, and I have *come down to deliver* them from the Egyptians...'" God knew their pain and suffering. God suffered with them. And God responded by calling Moses.

God didn't ask Moses; God simply told him. In the story, Moses was not too keen to undertake this mission. I love what this story says about Moses? Moses is totally believable. Moses had feelings of inferiority and all kinds of excuses why God could do better. 'Couldn't God send someone else? Who would believe him? He wasn't a very good speaker.' I can identify with Moses. Moses was reluctant to go, to say yes to God. But he did, and his life was changed forever. Just like Moses, God is here today, and God is calling you. We don't have a burning bush, but God is here just the same.

We find ourselves all over this story, don't we? The name Moses means, drawn out of the water. We too, have been drawn out of the waters of baptism, called to share God's love with others. We do that as husbands and wives, as parents, as employees and employers, as students and teachers. We respond to the call as citizens promoting the common good, working for peace and justice, responding with compassion to the needs around us. We respond to God's call when we care for the environment God has made. There are so many ways we can respond to God's call in our lives.

What about you? Have you ever felt that God was calling you to love and impact the lives of others. Many people feel that way about their jobs. A while back, I was making hospital visits I saw a medical tech wearing a shirt that said on the back, "This is our calling." For him, it wasn't just a job. Being a part of a healing profession is a way of living out God's calling in our lives. I know this is the way many teachers feel about what they do. It isn't just a job, a paycheck. It is a calling, a way of life, a way of touching the lives of others with help and compassion.

I visited someone in the hospital who had a life-threatening aneurysm. He told me how the experience had given him a new perspective on life. But he wasn't ready to die. "I just feel that

God has something left for me to do with my life." What about you? Is there something God wants you to do with your life? Maybe God is calling you to do something. Maybe you've been resisting God, like Moses, saying "God, could you please send someone else?" Some of you have said yes to God's call, even in times when you've had a little fear. Sometimes God's call will push us out of our comfort zone, just as it did for Moses. But when we say yes, God's call always brings great blessing into our lives.

Just like Moses, God is calling us to ministry in his name. Did you notice that this was where Moses learned God's name? "I am what I am." We could also translate it, "I will be what I will be." God is a god of action. And when people suffer, God jumps into action, calling God's people to mission. This is what God has done for us in Jesus Christ. God came to earth, took on flesh, suffered and died on the cross to show us how much God loves us and to rescue us from our sins. That's the good news we are called to share, even when we are reluctant, and even when we feel inadequate. Because it's not about us, it's all about God and God's love for people. And that love needs to be shared. It's not an impossible mission — not when God calls you, not for Moses, and not for you.

God is here today, not in a burning bush, but in the needs of the Hurricane Harvey victims, and in the needs of our neighbor across the street. God is calling your name. Listen. Can you hear it?

3. The Song — "Canticle Of The Turning"

What Next?

I Love To Preach The Story is 3-part work covering years A, B and C of the Revised Common Lectionary.
- Year A — Stories Of Origin
- Year B — Lessons In Leadership
- Year C — A Summer Of Prophet Sharing

If you and your congregation enjoyed exploring the stories in this book this summer, consider taking them through the other summer series. You will find that these ancient stories continue to speak with power and relevance today. And as a busy pastor, you will also discover that having a series during the summer will bring some focus and direction to your preaching.

Many pastors are part of a local text study group. But choosing a series idea like this might leave you on your own as most study groups often focus on the gospel lesson. So why not join an online study group? Social media is a powerful tool to share ideas. Consider joining a Facebook group to share how you adapted and contextualized your series. Do a search on Facebook for the group, "I Love to Preach the Story." There are three groups for each of the three years. Let's encourage each other and share our insights with one another. And if you would like to communicate with the author directly, you can send email to rolfsvanoe@gmail.com.

Blessings on your summer journey through these stories.

For as the rain and the snow come down from heaven, and do not return there until they have watered the earth, making it bring forth and sprout, giving seed to the sower and bread to the eater, so shall my word be that goes out from my mouth; it shall not return to me empty, but it shall accomplish that which I purpose, and succeed in the thing for which I sent it (Isaiah 55:10-11).

Ingram Content Group UK Ltd.
Milton Keynes UK
UKHW040815200723
425492UK00001B/161

9 780788 030468